T0330847

BEYOND THE EMERGENCY:
Development within UN Peace Missions

edited by
JEREMY GINIFER

Routledge
Taylor & Francis Group

LONDON AND NEW YORK

First published in 1997 in Great Britain by
Routledge
2 Park Square, Milton Park, Abingdon, Oxon, OX14 4RN
270 Madison Ave, New York NY 10016

Transferred to Digital Printing 2007

British Library Cataloguing in Publication Data:

A catalogue record for this book is available from the British Library.

ISBN 0 7146 4760 8 (cloth)
ISBN 0 7146 4321 1 (paper)

Library of Congress Cataloging-in-Publication Data:

A catalog record for this book is available from the Library of Congress.

This group of studies first appeared in a Special Issue on
[Beyond the Emergency: Development within UN Peace Missions] in
[*International Peacekeeping*, Vol.3, No.2 (Summer 1996)],
published by Routledge

Publisher's Note
The publisher has gone to great lengths to ensure the quality of this reprint
but points out that some imperfections in the original may be apparent

Contents

Notes on Contributors

Chris Alden is a Lecturer in International Relations in the University of the Witwatersrand, South Africa. He is the author of *Apartheid's Last Stand: the Rise and Fall of the South African Security State* (Macmillan, 1996), co-editor of *Afrique du Sud: Le Cap de Bonne Esperance* (Temps Modernes, 1995) and *Paris, Pretoria and the African Continent: the International Relations of States and Societies in Transition* (Macmillan, 1996). He has published on African politics, the UN and regional security issues.

Jeremy Ginifer is Deputy Director of the UN Programme at the Norwegian Institute of International Affairs (NUPI), Oslo, and also a Visiting Research Fellow at the Mountbatten Centre for International Studies, University of Southampton, UK. He is currently working on development within UN peace missions, disarmament and demobilization operations within southern Africa and identity politics in internal conflicts. His recent publications have concentrated on peacekeeping and humanitarianism in Africa.

Omar Halim is currently a Research Associate at the Centre for Strategic and International Studies, Jakarta, Indonesia. In his 28-year service with the United Nations, he worked in the Department of International Economic and Social Affairs, the Department of Public Information, the Department of Political Affairs, and the Department of Peacekeeping Operations. During the last seven of these years he served in peacekeeping missions in Namibia, Lebanon, Somalia and Liberia.

Assis Malaquias is the Executive Director of the Angola Institute in Washington, DC, and an Associate Researcher at the Centre for Foreign Policy Studies, Dalhousie University, Halifax. His current research focuses on transitions to democracy in African countries, including the prospects for sustainable democratic development in Angola.

Donald Rothchild is Professor of Political Science at the University of California, Davis. He is the author of *Racial Bargaining in Independent Kenya* and co-author of *Politics and Society in Contemporary Africa*. His latest co-authored book is *Sovereignty as Responsibility: Conflict Management in Africa*.

Timothy M. Shaw is Professor of Political Science and International Development Studies and Director of the Centre for Foreign Policy Studies at Dalhousie University. He has recently published articles on Africa's political economy in *Africa Today, European Journal of Development Research, International Journal* and *Mershon International Studies Review*. He has been a faculty member at universities in Nigeria, South Africa, Uganda, Zambia and Zimbabwe, and serves as General Editor of the Macmillan/St. Martin's Press International Political Economy Series.

Hugo Slim is Director of the Centre for Development and Emergency Planning (CENDEP) at the Oxford Brookes University. As well as writing on development issues, he has worked in humanitarian emergencies for the United Nations and the Save the Children Fund in Ethiopia, Sudan, Bangladesh and Iraqi Kurdistan.

Stephen John Stedman is an Associate Professor of African Studies at the Johns Hopkins University School of Advanced International Studies and a visiting scholar at the Center for International Security and Arms Control at Stanford University. He is currently writing on American foreign policy and internal conflicts in the post-Cold War period; the problem of 'spoilers' in peace processes; and conflict resolution in civil wars. He is the author of *Peacemaking in Civil War: International Mediation in Zimbabwe, 1974–1980* and co-author of *The New Is Not yet Born: Conflict Resolution in Southern Africa*.

J. David Whaley is currently the first Resident Co-ordinator of the Operational Activities for Development of the United Nations System and Resident Representative of the United Nations Development Programme (UNDP) in South Africa. He has extensive experience in the management of international development co-operation in Africa, having served as Resident Co-ordinator and Resident Representative in Benin (1979–84), in Algeria (1984–88) and in Kenya (1992–95). In 1988 and 1990 he served as Director for Operational Activities of the Office of the Director General for International Co-operation and Development.

Preface

The essays in this volume focus on the issue of development within the UN peace mission. It examines a number of critical issues relating to the interface between development, relief and peacekeeping, including institutional co-ordination, the implementation of development and peacebuilding in the field, with particular reference to Africa, and the contending philosophies that sometimes underpin military and developmental approaches to human security. Not least, it poses the question of how sustainable development fits within the post-conflict 'space' of UN peace missions. These missions, and increasingly humanitarianism, have tended to focus in the 1990s on short-term emergency aid and military security issues. Important as these are, there is a growing need to think long-term – beyond the emergency – and consider how to implement developmental strategies that allow war-torn societies to rebuild on a sustainable basis.

This volume draws on a series of presentations made at the seminar *Beyond the Emergency: Development within UN Peace Missions,* held in Pretoria on 13–14 March 1996, by the Norwegian Institute of International Affairs (NUPI) and the Institute for Defence Policy (IDP), and supported by the Norwegian Agency for Development Co-operation (NORAD). The editor thanks all three organizations for their support and the authors who worked so hard to produce excellent articles within tight deadlines. Thanks are also due to Michael Pugh, editor of *International Peacekeeping,* for his help with this book.

INTRODUCTION AND OVERVIEW

Development and the UN Peace Mission: A New Interface Required?

JEREMY GINIFER

Development has increasingly become a function of the UN peace mission during the 1990s. However, it has tended to be overshadowed in a number of missions by military security and emergency relief issues. The proposition explored in this article is that a greater developmental emphasis during UN missions may be productive in terms of bringing about durable peace processes. However, this implies that development needs to be 'recast' in terms of its positioning within UN conflict resolution and peace missions. Development has not been coherently conceptualized within UN conflict resolution, and military security and political modes of thinking have tended to prevail in peace missions. If development is to assume a central role in conflict prevention and resolution, problematic issues relating to contending philosophical, institutional and implementational approaches within the UN Secretariat will need to be addressed.

The importance of development is frequently stressed within UN peace missions. However, there appears to be something of a gap between this rhetoric and the reality of UN missions. It continues to be the 'emergency' and peacekeeping, and their imperatives, that characteristically dominate the UN mission. Emergency relief and security corner the lion's share of resources, and it is usually the political-military leadership that has the principal say in directing and shaping the course of peace operations. Proponents of development, such as non-governmental organizations (NGOs) and some UN organizations, are increasingly questioning whether this is the most efficacious approach to the challenge of creating lasting solutions to the endemic internal conflicts that confront the UN.

This article examines these issues, and in particular focuses on what might be termed the historical neglect of development within UN conflict resolution thinking. In so doing, it maps out the theoretical and operational contribution development can make to the prevention and resolution of conflicts. It is suggested that developmental approaches offer novel and potentially durable solutions to the addressing of underlying causes of conflicts, which in the past UN peace missions have not always utilized. Development stresses such notions as long-term engagement, reform and human and social approaches to the attaining of peace and security that are

Jeremy Ginifer is Deputy Director of the UN Programme at the Norwegian Institute of International Affairs, Oslo.

contrary to the traditional diplomatic and military instruments that were applied in peace missions. These sought, less ambitiously, to avert and contain conflict, rather than change behaviour or conditions underpinning conflicts.

Since the late 1980s and during the 1990s an awareness of the important role development can play within the UN peace mission has emerged. Such operations as ONUSAL in El Salvador and ONUMOZ in Mozambique, for example, were premised on the assumption that the stimulation of development was central to lasting peace processes. However, in practice, the integrating of development into the UN peace mission has posed a number of institutional, philosophical and implementational challenges which have arguably yet to be coherently resolved. Certainly, the concept of an integral mission, incorporating peacekeeping, emergency aid and development, has yet to be fully realized in the field; not least because the linking of strategies has proved extremely difficult to implement.

This article then seeks to map out the relevance of development in resolving conflicts and sustaining peace and raises the problematic issues that arise when two fundamentally differing conceptions of security (military/diplomatic and developmental) are fused into a holistic mission.

Mapping out Development

What is development? Duffield defines it as:

> a normative process of becoming: a series of interconnecting movements leading from poverty and vulnerability to security and well-being.[1]

While Anderson and Woodrow refer to:

> a process through which people's physical/material, social/organizational and motivational/attitudinal vulnerabilities (or capacities) are reduced (or increased).[2]

It is clear from these definitions that development is something qualitatively different from other forms of humanitarianism, such as emergency aid. While aid primarily seeks to preserve life or lessen suffering (although long-term linking strategies to development are frequently now a feature of aid) development seeks to change the underlying conditions of life. However, unlike aid, increasingly development is suffering from government cutbacks and resources are being diverted to emergency aid. This trend is even apparent within NGOs. In 1994, at least 10 per cent of total public development aid (US$8 billion) was disbursed by NGOs and almost half of this was accounted for by emergency relief, a trend which is continuing.[3]

Within the UN mission itself the disparity between emergency relief and development is particularly marked. In 1992, 39 per cent (US$4.09 billion) of total UN expenditure was given to 'emergency work in peacekeeping and humanitarian assistance', while US$774.4 million went to development.[4]

Further, the very concept of development as an efficacious response to crises is coming under attack. Antonio Donati of the Department of Humanitarian Affairs (DHA), for example, has noted that at the level of international consensus 'development no longer seems to be a mobilizing paradigm, but a new one has yet to emerge.'[5] Similarly, Rieff comments that the traditional development strategy of government-to-government aid, and its successor, an NGO-based strategy, have failed and 'there is no going back'.[6] However, this growing scepticism regarding development in some quarters obscures the fact that it offers a number of distinctive and potentially effective approaches to conflict prevention and resolution. First, development attempts to address the root causes of conflict, rather than reacting to its manifestations. Developmentalists argue that conflicts have their genesis in underdevelopment. At the least it seems reasonable to surmise that a causal connection exists between conflict and poverty. The fact that Africa, for example, has 33 of the 47 least developed countries in the world and the highest incidence of conflict in the world is suggestive of a linkage. It may be argued that through the alleviating of poverty and depredation sources of dysfunctional behaviour that underpin conflicts may be ameliorated. In turn, the development process theoretically stimulates the emergence of social and political structures conducive to more consensual, less violent forms of living, such as good governance/democracy.

Secondly, development is a constant – it is a long-term project which can take place before, during and following conflicts, rather than by intercession at a specific crisis point.[7] This once again potentially holds out the prospect of building a more sustainable peace.

Development and UN Conflict Resolution

The conceptual underpinnings of development and its 'positioning' within UN conflict resolution remains largely unexplored. The peacekeeping research community, for example, has tended to display an interest in development only when it has interfaced with military security issues, such as demobilization. This neglect has its foundation in the fact that UN conflict resolution has characteristically focused on the prevention and containment of conflict through military and diplomatic means; a classic instrument being the peacekeeping mission invented in the 1950s. What happened after the peacekeeping mission, and how the economic and social needs of individuals and peoples caught up in conflict could be met was largely regarded as outside the mission remit during the Cold War, in part because statist sovereignty issues largely precluded a more activist approach. At the same time, an artificial separateness developed between UN institutions involved in development – such as the United Nations Development Programme (UNDP) – and the Departments of Political Affairs and Peacekeeping.

While peacekeeping missions during the 1960s, the 1970s and the 1980s sometimes took on peacebuilding tasks, which included development, they remained dominated conceptually and operationally by military-diplomatic modes of thinking. These still exert considerable influence within the Secretariat, despite the increasing awareness of the need for multifaceted operations. This raises the question of whether UN peace mission strategy and planning are sufficiently developmental, despite the facts that linkages have been formed between the Department of Peacekeeping Operations (DPKO), the DHA and the UNDP in New York and Geneva,[8] and field co-operation in the form of regular briefings and consultation is a feature of many recent missions.[9]

It is instructive that conflict resolution parlance tends not to use the word development, but more usually refers to peacebuilding.[10] Peacebuilding has subtly different connotations from development, although the two concepts are clearly closely related. Further, the lack of an articulation of development within UN conflict resolution is reflected in Chapters VI and VII of the Charter, referring to the pacific settlement of disputes and international peace and security, which do not mention development, although elsewhere in Chapter IX, Article 55, and Chapter I, Article I, for example, development is described as a UN goal.[11] This tendency to relegate development to the fringes of UN conflict resolution in favour of military security was recently recognized by the Secretary-General, who noted that:

> Beset by the growth of conflicts, and the necessity to maintain the peace in the tense post-cold war world environment, we risk getting lost in the urgency of peacekeeping, at the expense of the longer term development effort.[12]

There appears to be an increasing realization that conflicts are unlikely to be resolved by short-term expedient responses and that the international community is faced with important choices. It can either choose to abandon substantive attempts to reconstitute war-torn societies and resort to minimalist forms of intervention, such as classic peacekeeping, or it will need to become more long-term in its approach. If the latter, it is apparent that there are still structural and philosophical impediments within the UN system that make it extremely difficult to pursue developmental agendas effectively . How these may be resolved is extremely problematic.

Development Problems in the UN Peace Mission

A series of problems and tensions may be discerned in the UN's attempts to pursue development and peace-building operationally. These include:

- a lack of effective institutional co-ordination and co-operation, both at a structural and a field level;

- contending developmental strategies: are 'top-down' or 'bottom-up' approaches most efficacious (or are both required?); and

- tensions between short-term versus sustainable approaches in the field, and failures to achieve relief and development linkages.

These problems persist, despite the fact that the UN has made considerable efforts to make its missions more developmental, holistic and integrated during the 1990s. UN missions, such as ONUMOZ, ONUSAL and Somalia (UNOSOM II), for example, attempted to improve on the perceived shortcomings of previous ones. They were informed, at least in principle, by an awareness of the linkages between the mission elements and the necessity of undertaking long-term development and peace-building if they were to achieve lasting results. However, in practice they found it difficult to implement developmental mandates. Given that the developmental mission is essentially a new venture this is not surprising; nevertheless, it remains a matter of concern.

Institutional Co-ordination and Co-operation

One of the most serious structural flaws has been the lack of policy co-ordination between the Secretariat and the Bretton Woods institutions. In effect, the organizations have sometimes been pursuing contradictory developmental policies. Willett notes that in Mozambique there was conflict between the human development agendas – fostered by the peace mission and the UN system generally – and the structural adjustment and macro-economic policies pursued by the World Bank and the International Monetary Fund.[13] The latter created increased hardship and dislocation within Mozambique, which threatened a return to violence, and a negation of the advances made by the peace mission.

Similarly, in El Salvador, de Soto notes that:

> The adjustment programme and the stabilization plan, on the one hand, and the peace process, on the other, were born and reared as if they were children of different families.[14]

The World Bank did not keep the UN abreast of its economic programme, while the UN neglected to inform the Bretton Woods institutions of the peace accords. This suggests that the relationship between the Secretariat and the Bretton Woods institutions needs to be rethought if development within peace missions is to be coherently implemented. This could include the systematic exchange of information and the integration of goals and activities, along with flexibility in the application of financial rules when peace-building/development requires it.[15]

Equally seriously, within the UN system itself there remains institutional competition, overlaps and poor co-ordination among key organizations involved in development within peace missions. It is beyond the scope of this article to examine this complex area in detail, but critics point to the disparate, decentralized nature of the UN humanitarian response system in general and the lack of a clear, authoritative leadership established in a single agency. Particularly controversial is the role of the DHA, which was set up to strengthen the co-ordination of humanitarian emergency assistance and also to manage the relief-development transition. It is claimed that the DHA has been slow to make the most of its resources and mandate. Slim comments that it:

> has made disappointing progress: it has fallen short of expectations, and missed the opportunity to reform significantly the UN approach to complex emergencies...an effective model of co-ordination...has yet to be constructed and implemented in a concerted fashion.[16]

Others note that the DHA operates under considerable constraints, not least the:

> separatism and built-in competition that is so pervasive in the UN system even in the face of the human desperation of emergencies.[17]

However, it is suggested that a restructuring of the DHA and closer teamwork between senior officials in development, political affairs and peacekeeping is required.[18] The DHA has pointed to its close links to UNDP and relief organizations in the relief/rehabilitation/reconstruction continuum,[19] and its dialogue with the DPA, DPKO and other UN organizations in the areas of preventive action, early warning information and so forth. Nevertheless, many critics think that without a fundamental rethinking of development co-ordination UN peace missions will continue to underperform in development.

Developmental Strategies: 'Top-down' or 'Bottom-up'?

A tension exists between the political/military and the developmental components as to the most efficacious method to stimulate development. The former has tended to temperamentally gravitate towards top-down approaches, such as the reconstituting of government, the strengthening of administrative structures and the rebuilding of infrastructure, as essential first steps towards the rebuilding of a war-torn society. While it is recognized that grass-roots initiatives, for example, may be called for, these have not tended to loom large in military/political planning. Unsurprisingly, soldiers and political officers have been particularly concerned with the restoration or establishment of order and authority as initial conditions for development to take place. In contrast, developmentalists have tended to stress individualistic and social initiatives at the local or the regional level. This has led them to be particularly critical of the leadership of a number of missions, not least that of the Somalia mission. A major factor, it has been suggested, in the failure of UNOSOM to stabilize Somalia was the top-down focus of dealing with the warlords and factional leaders, rather than more traditional leaders and structures.[20] Successes in building local structures – much of the work done by Somalis – was thrown into jeopardy by this approach, according to those working on the ground in development. Between May 1993 and February 1994, for example, 56 district councils and 40 councils had been provided with basic training, but:

> This promising bottom-up approach to rebuilding society was interrupted and held back when the UN leadership in Mogadishu... concentrat[ed] all its political efforts on the political factions and warlords...even the training programme had to be stopped for a whole year so that nothing would disturb negotiations between the factional leaders.[21]

Similarly, it is alleged that the only examples of successful reconciliation in Somalia occurred at the local and the regional level, and when grass-roots institutions were recognized and assisted rather than marginalized. Other critics of the mission go further and allege that, not only did the mission fail to consolidate at a grass-roots level, it also failed to conserve and strengthen government structures at the top.

The relative weights to be accorded to bottom-up and top-down approaches remains a point of doctrinal contention within UN missions. In an integrated mission, a theoretical case may be made for a dual-track approach, but how, and the extent to which this can be practicably implemented remains problematic.

Short-termism versus Sustainability

Inevitably, individual mission components have differing perceptions of developmental timespans. Developmental organizations may be engaged in a country for years and see development as a long-term project, while the military have shorter timescales frequently imposed by national governments or mandates. The fact that highly ambitious and complex missions in Somalia and Cambodia, for example, were assigned only several years for completion may be seen as emanating from political rather than developmental considerations. Further, the military tend to be culturally orientated towards the achievement of clearly stipulated tasks, while developmental tasks are frequently less tangible. These differing objectives and cultures have led to misunderstandings. In Mozambique, for example, clashes could be discerned between the, 'culture of peacekeeping versus development', particularly in implementing the demobilization of former combatants.[22] While the UN agencies stressed the long-term educational approach in the assembly places where demobilization was initiated, the peacekeepers had to focus on the more immediate technical task of making demobilization work smoothly, and ensuring that assembled soldiers did not take up arms again.[23] Both roles were clearly important – if the assembly place process collapsed Mozambique risked a return to armed conflict; on the other hand, without some form of long-term educational process, the gains might prove to be short-lived. As Bertram puts it, there may be inherent tensions between peacemakers and peace-builders, when the former are principally concerned with 'securing an end to the bloodshed', while the latter are concerned with 'securing the necessary conditions for a sustainable and democratic peace'.[24]

Conclusion

This article has suggested that new thinking is required in order to recast the role of development within UN conflict resolution and peace missions. It has further been postulated that development has certain unique attributes that provide novel approaches to conflict prevention and resolution. However, to contend that development in itself can provide comprehensive answers to the complex emergencies and societal conflicts that characterize the 1990s would be oversimple. Indeed, some critics of development have gone as far as to argue that the concept, infused as it is with mechanistic perceptions of social progress, is redundant in many intra-state contexts. The very notion that development is sustainable in a world of complex emergencies has been challenged. Duffield, for example, notes that:

> Developmentalism rests on the assumption of the universality of social progress. It is part of the myth of modernity. That is, the certainty that shared progress is the normal and long-term direction of all social change.[25]

Nor are the developmental organizations involved in peace missions any more paragons of virtue than other mission elements when it comes to their performance at UN headquarters or in the field. Examples of muddled thinking, disengagement from agreed mission objectives and the inability to co-ordinate their activities with other humanitarians and the military, can readily be identified.

However, perhaps the fundamental question that underpins the issue of development within UN missions needs to be reiterated: are two fundamentally differing conceptions (the military/political and the developmental) of how human security should be arrived at reconcilable? Does the UN, in fact, have the right strategy in place in attempting to seek synergies between these contending approaches? Two principal conceptual approaches to the developmental peace mission may identified. First, the integrated approach described above: this seeks to combine military security, relief, rehabilitation and development into a multifaceted operation, which attempts remedial measures across a broad range of levels – a kind of 'shotgun' approach.

Second, a contending method may be postulated: the atomistic approach. This would reject multifaceted operations in favour of dedicated missions. A dedicated developmental mission might forgo peacekeeping, for example, and concentrate purely on bottom-up developmental strategies. Such a mission could primarily involve civilian direction and be implemented by UN humanitarian organizations and NGOs.

Some observers believe that such an approach would require new and dedicated UN mechanisms. Erskine and Urquhart, for example, suggest that a UN Humanitarian Security Police be constituted to protect UN and NGO personnel, their transport and supplies.[26] It has also been suggested that if the UN is going to take peace-building really seriously it requires the creation of a highly professional and tenured UN peace-building service.

Whether the integrated or the atomistic approach is the more appropriate in developmental terms is open to debate – it may be the case that each has relevance in particular circumstances. However, it seems highly likely that the former will continue to prevail for the immediate future. The fact that peacekeeping is the activity funded under assessed contributions while development relies on voluntary contributions suggests a continuation of present arrangements, with the military element at the forefront.

A further point of considerable relevance is that approaches to the reconstituting of war-torn societies and complex emergencies have by necessity to be multifaceted. To have a realistic chance of alleviating conflicts, a range of measures are required, which tackle both the underlying causes of conflict and its immediate manifestations. Without feeding starving populations, protecting them from violence and putting structures in place that make life sustainable, there is little hope of achieving development. Conversely, the achieving of physical security will have long-term relevance only if it is allied with development. However, without a greater emphasis on developmental practice and some of the philosophical precepts that underpin development, the UN is unlikely to arrive at a sophisticated, workable understanding of what it takes to reconstitute war-torn societies.

NOTES

1. Mark Duffield, 'Complex Emergencies and the Crisis of Developmentalism', in Simon Maxwell and Margaret Buchanan-Smith (eds.), *Linking Relief and Development*, Vol.25, No.4, Oct. 1994, Brighton: Institute of Development Studies, p.38.
2. M. Anderson and P. Woodrow, *Rising from the Ashes: Development Strategies in Times of Disaster*, Boulder, CO: Westview Press, 1989, p.12., in Duffield (n.1), p.19.
3. Thomas G. Weiss, 'Military-Civilian Humanitarianism: the "Age of Innocence" Is Over', *International Peacekeeping*, Vol.2, No.2, Summer 1995, p.162.
4. See Susan Willett, 'Ostriches, Wise Old Elephants and Economic Reconstruction in Mozambique', *International Peacekeeping*, Vol.2, No.1, Spring 1995, p.44.
5. Eva Kaluzynska, 'Humanitarian Aid: Quality, Not Quantity Wanted', *The Courier*, No.154, Nov./Dec. 1995, p.90.
6. David Rieff, 'The Humanitarian Trap', *World Policy*, Vol.12, No.4, Winter 1995–96, p.10.
7. See Åge Eknes and Carsten Rønnfeldt, 'Development versus Peacekeeping', unpublished paper, Olso: Norwegian Institute of International Affairs, May 1995, pp.6–7.
8. See 'The DHA/DPKO/DPA Framework for Co-ordination', draft doc., 27 July 1995, New York: United Nations.
9. For an elaboration of some of the difficulties of co-ordination at the field level in Somalia, see, for example, Jarat Chopra, Åge Eknes and Toralv Nordbø, 'Fighting for Hope in Somalia', Oslo: Norwegian Institute of International Affairs Report, No.6, 1995, pp.72–88.
10. For an analysis of the conceptual parameters of peacebuilding see Michael Pugh, 'Peacebuilding as Developmentalism: Concepts from Disaster Research', *Contemporary Security Policy*, Vol.16, No.3, 1995, pp.320–46.
11. Chapter IX, Article 55 states that the UN shall:

    promote…higher standards of living, full employment, and conditions of economic and social progress and development.

    While Chapter I, Article 1 states that one of the UN's purposes is:

    To achieve international co-operation in solving international problems of an economic, social, cultural or humanitarian character.

12. Boutros Boutros-Ghali, *An Agenda for Development*, New York: Department of Public Information, United Nations, 1995, p.1.
13. See Willett (n.4), p.35.
14. Alvaro de Soto and Graciana del Castillo, 'Obstacles to Peacebuilding', *Foreign Policy*, No.94, Spring 1994, p.72.
15. For detailed suggestions regarding reform of UN/Bretton Woods co-ordination see ibid., pp.78–83.
16. Hugo Slim and Angela Penrose, 'UN Reform in a Changing World: Responding to Complex Emergences', in Joanna Macrae and Anthony Zwi (eds.), with Mark Duffield and Hugo Slim, *War and Hunger: Rethinking International Responses to Complex Emergencies*, London: Zed Books/Save the Children Fund (UK), 1994, p.202.
17. Erskine Childers with Brian Urquhart, 'Renewing the United Nations System', *Development Dialogue*, No.1, 1994, p.113.
18. Ibid., pp.203–4.
19. Michael Askwith, 'The Roles of DHA and UNDP in Linking Relief and Development', in Maxwell and Buchanan-Smith (n.1), p.103.

20. See Sture Normark, 'Building Local Political Institutions: District and Regional Councils', paper to the Comprehensive Seminar on Lessons Learned from the United Nations Operation in Somalia, Lessons-Learned Unit, Department of Peacekeeping Operations, Plainsboro, NJ, 13–15 Sep. 1995, p.3.
21. Ibid., p.8.
22. Winrich Kuhne, Bernhard Weimer and Sabine Fandrych, International Workshop on the Successful Conclusion of the United Nations Operation in Mozambique (ONUMOZ), report, New York: Friedrich Ebert Foundation and the Stiftung Wissenschaft und Politik, 27 Mar. 1995, p.9.
23. Ibid., p.9.
24. Eva Bertram, 'Reinventing Governments: the Promise and Perils of United Nations Peacebuilding', *Journal of Conflict Resolution*, Vol.39, No.3, Sep. 1995, p.396.
25. Duffield (n.1), p.38.
26. Childers and Urquhart (n.17), p.204.

CONCEPTUAL ISSUES

Peace Operations: From Short-Term to Long-Term Commitment

STEPHEN JOHN STEDMAN and
DONALD ROTHCHILD

By developing a strategic approach to the implementation of peace accords in civil war, the United Nations can better the odds for ending a war and fostering development in the long run. Recent attempts at implementation have suffered from recurring difficulties: incomplete, vague and expedient agreements; lack of co-ordination between mediators and those who have to implement an agreement; lack of co-ordination between implementing agencies; lack of sustained attention by the international community; incomplete fulfilment of agreements by warring parties; and the presence of 'spoilers' who seek to destroy any incipient peace. To overcome these difficulties, the UN must encourage the parties to choose political, cultural, social and economic security-building measures during the negotiation phase and systematically apply confidence-building measures to the military components of implementation. This demands a reconsideration of peace making in a civil war to include a long-term international commitment to the development of war-torn societies.

According to a number of accounts, UN peacekeeping is on its deathbed and desperately needs resuscitation. Analysts disagree, however, about the nature of its affliction. Alan James suggests that the UN fell victim to over-ambition by trying to make peace in civil wars – conflicts that he describes as essentially unresolvable.[1] At the other extreme is David Rieff who, by confusing the UN performance in Bosnia with UN peacekeeping in general, has pronounced UN peacekeeping morally bankrupt owing to its lack of ambition.[2] A more balanced assessment would agree that UN peacekeeping is in crisis; partly because of over-use and underfunding and partly owing to its taking on unprecedented tasks in unprecedented situations; and partly because of the lack of fit between its traditional doctrine and its new commitments.[3] Even so, between 1989 and 1995, UN peacekeeping in fact brought three protracted civil wars to an end in Namibia, El Salvador and Mozambique.[4]

An objective assessment of UN peacekeeping since the end of the Cold

Stephen John Stedman is an Associate Professor of African Studies at the Johns Hopkins University School of Advanced International Studies and a visiting scholar at the Center for International Security and Arms Control at Stanford University; Donald Rothchild is Professor of Political Science at the University of California, Davis.

War suggests that, when certain basic requirements are met, peacekeeping has a chance of being effective. In cases where the parties to a conflict agree to end their war and commit themselves to a detailed framework for achieving peace, the success rate in ending wars has been 50 per cent (success in Namibia, El Salvador and Mozambique; failure in Rwanda, Cambodia and Angola). However, where the UN has failed at implementation the results have been catastrophic: many more people died in Angola and Rwanda *after* peace agreements failed than during the years of war that preceded them.

But even where implementation has succeeded – as in El Salvador and Mozambique – the countries have been so devastated by war that the long-term viability of peace remains in doubt. Indeed, researchers from differing theoretical perspectives agree that negotiated settlements of civil wars tend to be plagued by continued instability and often end in a reversion to violence.[5] If common sense prevailed in the world this would not be an insurmountable problem; having assisted countries in ending their long, bloody wars, the international community would show the far-sightedness to commit itself to their sustained reconstruction and development. Remarkably, this does not appear to be the case: the UN's member states have shown short-sightedness by reducing their commitment to countries crawling out from the carnage of civil war.[6]

This suggests two paramount challenges for peacekeeping today:

• to address the problem of short-term implementation of peace accords to prevent future Rwandas and Angolas; and,

• to address the relationship between short-term peacekeeping and long-term peace-building and development to ensure sustained peace in cases such as Mozambique.

The argument put forward here is that there are methods of implementing peace agreements in the short term that can maximize the long-term commitment by warring parties to those agreements. By creating a strategic approach to implementation, the UN can maximize the chances of ending the war in the short run and fostering development in the long run.

The key task of the short-term implementation of peace settlements is to provide means for parties to test their perceptions of each other, to reduce the risks of making peace, and to lessen the parties' fears of settlement. On the whole, UN implementation of settlements has approached such challenges neither in a strategic manner nor with an explicit doctrinal foundation. We argue here that UN implementation should draw explicitly and rigorously from the concepts of confidence-building and security-building.

Confidence-building relies on small, transparent mutual tests of commitment, supported by third-party verification of compliance and common forums where the parties can discuss their behaviour, motivations and perceptions. Confidence-building measures (CBMs) must be systematically established with regard to the military aspects of war termination: cease-fires; cantonment of soldiers; disarmament; demobilization; and force restructuring.

However, the attainment of peace after a civil war depends on more than the successful short-term implementation of a settlement. The long-term stability of agreements requires the creation of new institutions that provide incentives for, and an environment in which the parties may resolve on-going and new conflicts without resort to violence. Mediation and implementation, therefore, should have a dual purpose: to bring the immediate war to an end and to structure future relations in such a way as to facilitate a transition to what Adam Przeworski calls a 'self-enforcing' regime, one where:

> all the relevant political forces find it best to continue to submit their interests and values to the uncertain interplay of the institutions.[7]

CBMs are necessary, but not sufficient, to promote peace. As Johan Jorgen Holst, one of the founders of the concept of military CBMs, points out:

> confidence is the product of much broader patterns of relations than those which relate to military security. In fact, the latter have to be woven into a complex texture of economic, cultural, technical, and social relationships.[8]

The key ingredient in improving short-term commitment, and increasing the likelihood of long-term commitment, is the process of security-building. This involves measures to persuade warring parties and their followers to view peace as an extended and interconnected process that encompasses problem solving, negotiation, the implementation of agreements, and the creation and protection of valued political, cultural and economic relationships. When peace is viewed as an on-going process, then relationships of political exchange and reciprocity may bring about political learning among the rival parties and the expectation that co-operation will continue in the future.[9]

The first section of this article describes the problem of implementing peace agreements in civil wars and the role of the UN in assisting this. The second section describes six recurring problems that have negatively affected the UN's implementation of peace agreements. In the third and final section we discuss the need to approach the implementation of peace agreements systematically through confidence- and security-building, and what that will mean for the international commitment to making peace in civil wars.

Implementation of Peace Accords

Between 1991 and spring 1996, four civil wars were successfully negotiated, only to relapse into violence during the implementation phase: Cambodia, Liberia, Angola, and Rwanda.

The reasons for failed implementation follow direct from the characteristics of civil war.[10] Since fear is high and trust is low among antagonists, parties may fail to carry out their commitments in the belief that their adversary will take advantage of them.[11] Alternatively, since some leaders define the conflict in all-or-nothing terms, their commitment to the negotiated settlement may be tactical: to weaken their opponent and strengthen themselves. If the agreement promises to bring them to power, then they will meet their obligations. However, if the agreement looks as if it will reduce their power, they will go back to war – possibly launching a pre-emptive attack. Finally, since the organizational coherence of the warring parties may be in question, rogue factions on either side may try to destroy the agreement by undermining the implementation process.

Many international mediators assume that the signing of a peace agreement establishes that the warring parties have a mutual understanding of the stakes of implementation and a desire for peace over war.[12] Moreover, military planning to assist implementation is usually done on a best-case evaluation that assumes the basic good faith of the warring parties.[13] These assumptions are profoundly misleading. A more realistic assessment must consider the uncertainties inherent in implementation, of which there are four major sources.

First, the preferences of the warring parties are not common knowledge. The mere signing of a peace agreement does not imply that the parties prefer settlement to continuing the war. Parties in civil war may sign an agreement as a tactic: they buy time to gain strength during a cessation of hostilities and hope that their adversary will reveal weakness – all in order to take advantage of the settlement, return to war and attain complete victory.

Secondly, the pay-offs of implementing peace agreements are not common knowledge; no one knows for certain the rewards and costs associated with making peace, or returning to war. Many settlements use elections to establish in part the pay-offs of peace. However, since the winner and the loser in an election are not known in advance, the players are uncertain about the pay-offs regarding peace. A party may agree to a settlement only in the hope of winning an election; if the party loses the election, then it may prefer to return to war.

Parties in recent civil wars have even misjudged the pay-off for a unilateral return to war. The Presidential Guard in Rwanda believed that by taking advantage of the peace settlement it could win a complete victory and forge a final solution to the country's ethnic conflict. Instead, within two months – while it directed the killing of 800,000 civilians – its army was utterly routed by a smaller but better trained opponent. In Angola, Jonas Savimbi's Uniao Nacional para a Independência Total de Angola (UNITA) controlled nearly 80 per cent of the country during its post-election offensive of 1992, only to see the Angolan government regroup, rearm, hire South African mercenaries and gradually regain lost ground to the point where UNITA faced likely military defeat.

Thirdly, it is unclear what the act of cheating means during implementation. In every case of implementation of civil war settlements, cheating has taken place on all sides. Because everyone cheats, the motivation behind it is crucial to the success of the peace process. For example, an antagonist may keep arms and soldiers out of a cantonment area as a fail-safe move in case an opponent returns to war; or an antagonist may keep arms and soldiers out of a cantonment centre because they are useful for intimidating potential voters in the area. In such a case, the party may want the settlement to go forward, but will try to cheat to get a better outcome. On the other hand, a party may keep arms and soldiers out of a cantonment centre because its leader is waiting for the best opportunity to return to war in the hope of winning outright.

Fourthly, the lack of organizational cohesiveness of the warring parties may make it difficult to attribute an act of cheating to the party's leadership. In February and March 1980, during the implementation of the Lancaster House agreement in Zimbabwe-Rhodesia, Rhodesian special forces twice tried to assassinate the Zimbabwe African National Union (ZANU) leader Robert Mugabe, raising the issue of whether the forces had acted alone or under the command of their political bosses who signed the peace agreement.

Some analysts argue that the international community should judge the will of the combatants to make peace before it agrees to implement a peace agreement in civil war.[14] In retrospect, an observer might be able to judge that at the signing of an agreement the parties in Namibia and El Salvador, for example, were willing to make peace, but at the time that will was not evident, to either the participants or third parties.[15] In still other cases, where the evidence that the parties lacked the will to make peace seems overwhelming – Zimbabwe-Rhodesia in 1979 and Mozambique in 1993 – third-party pressures and incentives proved critical in maintaining momentum and, in the end, resulted in successful implementation.

The Role of the International Community

In the short term, negotiated settlements to civil wars mean an additional dangerous period of uncertainty and insecurity for the combatants. A key problem for antagonists – and third parties who attempt to oversee implementation – is imperfect information about the goals and character of their opponents. Are they sincere in wanting to make peace, or is their agreement only a tactic to try to win in the settlement what has been denied them on the battlefield? Even if all parties are sincere in wanting to make peace, their insecurity may lead them to pursue policies that are destructive of the mutual trust that is necessary for agreements to endure.

Negotiated settlements of civil wars provide opportunities for antagonists to reveal their preferences regarding peace. Implementation is the test of sincerity. But, unless the implementation phase is designed and administered well, the failure of the parties to live up to their commitments may reflect an inadequacy of the test, and not the lack of requisite sincerity.

The task of assisting implementation in peace agreements has fallen to the UN by default. Since 1989 it has helped to implement civil war agreements in Namibia, Western Sahara, Nicaragua, Angola, Cambodia, Mozambique, El Salvador and Rwanda. In so doing it has tried to graft its traditional approach to peacekeeping on to a large set of tasks that were not foreseen during the early years of UN peacekeeping.

To implement negotiated settlements in civil wars is a greater challenge than classic peacekeeping. It is similar to the latter in that the warring parties have signed an agreement to end hostilities. But whereas classic peacekeeping seeks only to monitor the separation of contending armies, peace settlements in civil war require the demobilization of forces and the creation of a unified army. Classic peacekeeping worked where peace agreements involved a static consolidation of borders and battle lines between states. Peace agreements in civil wars are inherently dynamic and therefore riskier and more difficult to monitor.

The UN can assist the implementation of peace agreements by addressing the uncertainties of the warring factions. By supplying information, monitoring and verifying compliance, and interpreting reluctance to meet obligations, it can clarify motives and reduce uncertainty about actor preferences and behaviour. It can also emphasize rules of conduct and encourage compliance, and the UN can try to convince the parties that there are costs in resuming war by appeals to regional and international sponsors.[16]

One misconception about the role of international actors in peace-agreement implementation needs to be put to rest: that the third party enforces or guarantees the peace agreement.[17] Scholars who imply that the third party will protect a disadvantaged party, or will use military force to gain compliance, distort what has happened in successful implementation. If the implementation of the El Salvador peace accords had broken down, for example, neither the UN nor the United States would have intervened militarily to enforce a settlement.

In the future, peace implementation forces may choose to use force to compel factions to implement their agreements. But the odds against successful coercion are long and must be calculated on:

- the effects on the targeted faction – whether it will back down or not – which in turn is likely to depend on what is demanded of the faction;
- what is demanded of the faction;[18]
- the effects on achieving other aspects of the mission's mandate, such as the delivery of humanitarian assistance or the holding of an election;
- the effects on troop-contributing countries (will they agree and form a unified front against the targeted faction?);
- the effect on the political consensus of the Security Council (SC) and interested countries (will they support the sustained use of violence, if necessary, to compel a faction?); and
- the judgement that, if an escalation of violence results, the international community will supply the will and necessary resources to gain escalation dominance.

Even when implementing forces choose to use compulsion to enforce peace it is a short-term option. Unless the implementing force is prepared to stay in a war-torn country in perpetuity the negotiated settlement, ultimately, must be self-enforced by the antagonists. That is why negotiated settlements of civil wars are so difficult and infrequent; the answer is not to provide external enforcement, but to think of ways to convince the parties to honour their commitments in the absence of external enforcement.

Difficulties of Implementation

The implementation of peace accords in civil wars must overcome six problems:

Spoilers

The biggest problem by far is getting parties who sign agreements to live up to their commitments. In Angola Jonas Savimbi, the leader of UNITA, returned to war when he lost the first round of elections in 1992. In Cambodia the Khmer Rouge reneged on the Paris Peace Accords almost immediately after signing them in 1992. In Rwanda the Juvenal Habyarimana government refused to implement key provisions of the Arusha Accords; when Habyarimana finally took steps to proceed with the peace plan he was assassinated by hard-line elements in his own military, who then plunged the country into genocide.

The UN, which was given the job of monitoring implementation in Angola, Cambodia and Rwanda, seemed incapable of responding to clear signals that one or both parties were cheating. This may be attributed, in part, to UN peacekeeping assumptions, which posit that to oppose transgressions opens UN operations to charges of bias.

Mediators, who have a vested interest and substantial investment of time, energy and honour in seeing settlements implemented, tend to interpret acts of non-compliance as motivated by fear rather than insincerity. Even if they interpret motivations as malign and admit that insincerity is involved they usually assert that the parties in question are trying to cheat to get better settlements, rather than attempting to destroy the settlements.

On the rare occasions when cheating is clearly recognized as such, the typical response by the international community is to reward the cheater – what is commonly referred to as 'appeasement'. In Cambodia the UN refused to confront Khmer Rouge and government violations of the peace accord and instead ignored transgressions, or used rewards to prompt compliance. In Rwanda the UN and the United States responded to genocide by urging the parties to return to the negotiating table. And in Angola United States policy went to great lengths to blame everything but Savimbi's desire for power as the reason for the failure of the peace process.

In Angola, Cambodia, and Rwanda appeasement was an ineffective and morally bankrupt policy. Appeasement cannot work if the targeted party interprets it as weakness. Critics of the UN operation in Cambodia believe that the failure of UN Special Representative Yasushi Akashi to challenge Khmer Rouge violations of the peace agreement:

> encouraged the KR to believe that it could get away with any abuse, no matter how blatant.[19]

Moreover, the appeasement of the Khmer Rouge:

> gave the other Cambodian parties an incentive to violate provisions of the Accords.[20]

The odds against appeasement working are long because of the societal and cultural contexts of civil wars. In civil wars the rule of law has broken down, force has become the ultimate arbiter of disputes, and accommodation can easily be interpreted as weakness.

Ideally, an implementing force must be strong and determined enough to insist that local parties must meet their obligations. If a party still refuses to carry out the peace accords the UN should call attention to the violation and establish that antagonists must adhere to rules. The willingness to take a tough line on violations must start at the beginning of an operation, when the reputation of the mission is being formed. Once lost, credibility and legitimacy are extremely difficult to re-establish.[21]

An obstacle to establishing a tough approach to implementation is the operational code that UN bureaucrats bring with them to missions. They tend to see the world in a legalistic not a strategic fashion.[22] They assume that local parties will act in good faith to meet their obligations. The UN emphasis on the importance of a good working relationship with all parties may be a barrier to confronting recalcitrant civil war leaders effectively.[23]

Incomplete, Vague or Expedient Agreements

Implementation of a given peace agreement is directly affected by the quality of the agreement. Incomplete agreements simply delay hard bargaining to the period of implementation, an inherently uncertain and dangerous time. For example, one US adviser to the Angolan peace talks of 1990-91 admitted that the demobilization and integration of armies was an afterthought to the successful negotiation of the Bicesse accords.[24] Unwilling to risk the progress made on other issues in the peace settlement and eager to generate momentum for peace, the mediators fudged the details of how demobilization and integration would take place. In the event, the UN was given a supervisory role for an ill-thought out process of demobilization, with few resources to monitor compliance. In essence, because the issue was left unnegotiated at Bicesse, the UN and its Special Representative in Angola, Margaret Anstee, had to take on the additional role of mediator at precisely the time when the UN had to implement the agreement.

Implementors also have to step into a mediating role when the provisions of an accord are vague. Unclear provisions open loopholes for warring parties to abuse. In Cambodia, for example, the provisions of the Paris Peace Accords were unclear as to the extent of UN authority during the implementation process. The Khmer Rouge argued that the UN had absolute authority and should render the SOC (State of Cambodia) simply one player among several. The SOC argued that the UN authority was in fact limited, and it resisted attempts by the UN to exert administrative control.

Finally, in some situations the provisions of agreements may be crystal clear, but counterproductive to stable implementation. Again, there was an uneasiness among the Bicesse accord mediators concerning the winner-take-all presidential electoral system and the lack of regional or federal institutions.[25] When both parties insisted that they wanted a winner-take-all system, the mediators, acting expediently, felt it best not to impose their own preferences. Although we do not want to excuse the decision by Jonas Savimbi to return to war in October 1992, there might have been a greater likelihood of his compliance if the agreement had provided more incentives for the party that lost the elections.

Poor quality agreements make it difficult for UN implementors to take a tough line against spoilers. First, as Ratner points out, a direct result of such a poor agreement is that the UN must simultaneously implement and mediate – roles that may conflict.[26] Because UN representatives in the field are commonly called upon to clarify vague sections of agreements, or called upon to add crucial details to incomplete agreements, they feel that they must guard their impartiality and neutrality in order to fulfil their role as mediators. Secondly, the fact that an agreement can be deemed vague or incomplete makes it difficult to make a clear, compelling judgement about who is a spoiler in any given case.

Incomplete Adherence to Agreements

Even where civil wars were brought to an end, as in Namibia, Mozambique, El Salvador, Nicaragua and Zimbabwe, many of the provisions of the peace accords were left unfulfilled in order to muddle through to an election. However, the failure to carry out all aspects of the accords has had dangerous implications for long-term stability in those countries. A failure to demobilize soldiers promptly and to provide them with adequate financial means may lead to continuing political instability, as happened in Zimbabwe in the 1980s; or may create large-scale banditry, a problem that has plagued Cambodia, El Salvador and Mozambique. Failure to disarm factions and to destroy stocks of weapons may create a thriving informal market in small arms, which may both prevent the establishment of law and order inside the country and destabilize others in the region, a problem that has plagued southern Africa.[27] A failure to meet provisions concerning land resettlement, as in El Salvador, may create new grievances which may incite new violence. A failure to insist on strict obediance to the rules of democratic competition, as was the case in El Salvador, may undermine party, and popular, confidence in democratic institutions as a means for fairly resolving conflicts. A failure to insist on the protection of human rights and the accountability of police, as in Cambodia, may undermine the prospects for popular confidence in a newly-elected government.

Poor Co-ordination between Mediating and Implementing Bodies

The prospects for successful implementation of negotiated settlements can be improved by better co-ordination between those who mediate settlements and the UN, which implements them. In many cases the warring parties have established timetables and logistical requirements that are impossible to meet. In Rwanda, UN approval of a mission to implement the Arusha Accords came nearly three months after the signing of the agreement. The number of soldiers sent to carry out the mission was 2,500 fewer than the warring parties expected. Moreover, their deployment was delayed until February 1994 – six months after the signing of the peace treaty.

In Mozambique, the parties created an implementation plan that called for the deployment of a large UN administrative and military presence, which was to begin assisting the demobilization effort in one month and carry out full demobilization, disarmament, the creation of a unified military, the repatriation of over six million displaced persons and hold elections – all in one year's time. This was supposed to occur in a country with little transportation and communication infrastructure. This plan, negotiated without the input of the individuals and organizations who would have to implement it, simply assumed that the UN would be willing and able to meet the requirements. In the event the UN mandate for the mission in Mozambique was not approved until two months after the peace agreement was signed; the first fully operational contingent of troops arrived five months later.

The international community's ability to assuage the fears of warring parties depends on the quick arrival and establishment of an implementation force.[28] The UN must be kept aware of demands that will be made of it in implementing peace agreements and plan accordingly. Member states must quickly authorize the resources and deployments needed to fulfil the mission and improvements must be made in contracting for delivery services.

Poor Co-ordination among UN Agencies during Implementation

The peace treaties that have successfully ended civil wars in the 1990s have been comprehensive documents that address a wide range of military, political, social and economic issues. Most have involved regional and international participation. The tendency of the UN has been to address these several components in an *ad hoc* way: peacekeepers have been sent to build military confidence; relief workers have been sent to address short-term humanitarian emergencies; development agencies have helped to address long-term social needs; human rights advocates have helped to educate populations about the need to foster and protect human rights; and representatives of international financial institutions have tackled budgetary and monetary problems. What has been lacking in many cases is effective co-ordination among these actors.

Alvaro de Soto, the UN mediator of the Salvadoran peace accords, argues that in war-torn societies international structural adjustment and stabilization policies often conflict with the implementation of peace plans in ways that keep both efforts from succeeding.[29] Peace settlements are more likely to succeed if money is provided to tackle the economic and social conditions that help to produce civil war and political instability. Reconstruction, land transfers, demobilization, and military, police and judicial reforms involve large expenses. However, international financial institutions simultaneously attempt to create the fiscal discipline necessary for long-term economic growth. Although peace and economic development are not independently sustainable, the international agencies tasked to achieve these goals operate at cross-purposes.[30]

This was apparent in Mozambique in October 1995, one year after the successful elections that ended the war in the country. Ambassadors of donor countries and the World Bank representative in Maputo rebelled against the policies of the International Monetary Fund (IMF), arguing that IMF austerity plans were imposing conditions that made reconstruction and development in Mozambique impossible.[31]

The Lack of 'Follow-through'

The problem of poor co-ordination could be more readily overcome if the international community would sustain assistance to countries that successfully implement peace agreements. Donors are often willing to promise aid and assistance while agreements are being negotiated and implemented but attention wanes and resources vanish when elections are held. Between 1991 and 1994, for example, donors pledged nearly US$1.7 billion to Cambodia; the actual assistance delivered was US$300–500 million.[32] In El Salvador, donors were quick to pledge support for the government's national reconstruction plan, but they have been slow in disbursing money. One year after the 1994 elections the government had to appeal to donors to help meet a shortfall of approximately US$158 million in financing for the peace accords.[33]

The sustenance of peace settlements depends on more than financial assistance from the international community. Drawing on the Cambodian experience, Findlay argues that international agencies should continue long-term security-building programmes between adversaries long after elections bring the formal peace process to a close.[34]

From Short to Long-Term Commitment

To overcome such difficulties will take a comprehensive rethinking of peacemaking in civil war: of what is at stake, and how short-term policies may affect long-term commitment. In addition, there will be need for a reorganization of UN peace operations to provide for strategic planning and the comprehensive delivery of services.[35]

A major step is to acknowledge that insecurity in civil war is a product of military, political, social and economic factors, and thus measures have to be taken to address all these factors. CBMs provide a useful approach to the problem of implementing key military provisions – such as cease-fires, demobilization and disarmament – while security-building measures provide a useful approach to the political, social and economic sources of insecurity.

CBMs

Although the concept of CBMs was developed in the international security and arms control literature of the 1970s and the 1980s, it can be fruitfully adapted to the challenge of peace implementation in civil wars. CBMs, in arms control parlance, refer to arrangements that:

> attempt to reduce or eliminate misperceptions about specific military threats or concerns by communicating adequately verifiable evidence of acceptable reliability to the effect that those concerns are groundless.[36]

In practice, arms control CBMs are limited, incremental, transparent, verifiable actions that demonstrate compliance with promises made through a treaty. Specifically, they usually involve information and communications measures to eliminate misperceptions about military action and constraining measures that aim to prevent military activities that may generate hostile misperceptions.[37] Confidence is built when a party believes that an adversary is fulfilling its obligations, that it is trustworthy and its intentions benign.

With slight modifications, the notion of CBMs may be applied to the implementation of peace agreements in civil wars. As stated earlier, the key military dilemma for warring parties in these wars stems from incomplete information about the preferences of adversaries: is their commitment to peace sincere or tactical? If it is tactical, then an opponent is likely to revert to war when it feels that the situation is advantageous. The process of implementing peace produces vulnerability and uncertainty. CBMs can reduce uncertainty by monitoring compliance with agreements and by establishing forums to investigate and clarify the intent behind potentially hostile actions. Further, CBMs can reduce vulnerability by breaking large-scale processes of demobilization, disarmament and the integration of forces into smaller, incremental, less threatening steps.

'Outsiders' can help to build confidence by verifying compliance with agreements. Verification entails 'a continuous process of monitoring and assessment', requiring technical collection, compliance assessment and compliance problem-solving. The interpretation of violations, especially what violations 'suggest about intentionality (e.g., the degree of deliberateness)' is critical to verification and confidence-building.[38]

As Schear notes, verification promotes compliance. First, verification helps to 'safeguard against deliberate violations' and to deter the deliberate evasion of peace-treaty provisions.[39] Secondly, by highlighting and acknowledging compliance, verification measures encourage parties to meet their obligations. Moreover:

> if jointly recognized and safeguarded, verification measures will add a degree of transparency to the military balance that could help to reduce the frictions arising from uncertainties and worst-case estimates of the other side's capability.[40]

As Schear observes, confidence-building involves the making of judgements regarding motives. Structured CBMs provide a forum:

> whereby each side can raise questions about the other's activities, clarify ambiguous behaviour or opposing interpretations of treaty language, and work out agreed understandings to avoid future problems or disagreements on obligations.[41]

The CBM approach to implementing peace agreements can avoid the trap of assuming that only fear and misperception divide the warring parties. Rather, by stressing visible, incremental compliance, it provides a means for the parties to reveal their preferences and intentions. The irony, of course, is that CBMs may produce evidence that demonstrates the futility of building confidence; they may reveal that a party is a spoiler that intends to destroy an agreement, rather than a fearful party that sincerely wants peace. In such circumstances the UN must have the courage and honesty to label a party a spoiler; if not, then the process of confidence-building itself may weaken a sincere party.

Security-building Measures

As stated earlier, the long-term achievement of peace in civil wars depends on more than the implementation of the military aspects of an agreement. The insecurity of warring parties and their followers involves political, social, cultural and economic concerns; the long-term commitment of factions to a peace process depends, in large part, on whether such concerns are met.

This acknowledgment, that the commitment of parties to peace involves aspects other than military security, has led some commentators to broaden the application of CBMs to non-military areas. While this may be fruitful, it is important that the key characteristics of CBMs are kept in mind. CBMs address the problem of how to signal benign intent, by stressing verifiable behaviour. Rhetorical commitments to peace, declarations of peacefulness, or even choices made in establishing an agreement cannot be regarded as

CBMs. Recent psychological experiments have confirmed what many have suspected: in situations of low trust, pronouncements of benign intentions are not enough to encourage co-operative responses.[42]

It is difficult to imagine exactly what a cultural or political equivalent to a military CBM might be. A political CBM would perhaps be election monitoring, where through verification parties may establish whether their opponents are living up to their promises to campaign lawfully. Another such measure might be an agreement for prior notification of political rallies to ensure that inadvertent violence was avoided. This kind of measure was a key component of the National Peace Accord in South Africa. A cultural CBM may be the avoidance of public ethnic or political 'hate rhetoric' – a commitment that can be monitored and verified.

However, in order to stress the need for parties to take steps that begin to address the non-military fears in civil wars, we emphasize the necessity of security-building measures. Such measures differ from CBMs in the following way: CBMs refer to verifiable behaviour that demonstrates the willingness of the parties to make peace; security-building measures, on the other hand, refer to institutional and policy choices, and verbal commitments that create expectations about future political, cultural, social and economic security. Security-building measures create a framework of rules and expectations, while CBMs create the trust for a continuing behavioral commitment within peace processes.

Political Security-building Measures

In order to prevent the unravelling of agreements, it is important for leaders to emphasize the notion of fairness towards all major interests throughout the peace process.[43] In this respect, democracy may be interpreted quite widely, embracing a number of the measures and principles of governance which lessen fear of any agreement among political minorities. Prominent among such security measures are: provisions on power-sharing; decentralization; cultural autonomy and respect for traditional authorities; proportional regional allocations; balanced recruitment into the civil service and army; competitive election systems; and demilitarization. Unless adversaries can deal with these issues effectively during the negotiation stage, there is a high probability that serious conflict will emerge during the complex bargaining encounters that will inevitably surface when the accords are put into effect.

Cultural Security-building Measures

The need for the new post-settlement state to interact in a sensitive manner with traditional authorities and local cultures is critical in establishing sustainable peace. Where a heavy-handed central government has dealt in a cavalier fashion with traditional leaders, as in the case of Frente de Libertação de Mocambique (FRELIMO) in Mozambique during the late 1970s and the early 1980s, the effect was to exacerbate tensions and promote resistance.[44] Similarly, efforts by the National Islamic Front government in Sudan to subsume other cultures by means of repressive laws on language, the practice of religion and the application of *Sharia* have proved largely counterproductive, leading to a defiant opposition and insurgency, as well as gravely weakening the Sudanese economy.

However, a tradition of respect for cultural leaders and local practices before the outbreak of civil war or during the negotiation phase has proved to be nurturing, helping to bring about a return to normality. In Mozambique, an increasingly pragmatic government has agreed to respect traditional authorities and has allowed them a symbolic role in local affairs.[45] In South Africa the 1993 Constitution made 11 languages official at the national level, while allowing a provincial legislature the right to declare any of these official for the whole or any part of the sub-region.[46] Moreover, President Mandela has urged his colleagues to exercise sensitivity on the touchy question of removing Afrikaner monuments. The effect of such cultural sensitivity is to provide an incentive for participation within the political system. Minority groups do not have to threaten secession or resort to violence and warfare to gain respect for their cultural identities; instead, their traditional authorities and cultures are safeguarded under the law of the land, eliminating a contentious issue from the public arena.

Economic Security Building

This refers to the creation of a belief that peace will pay; that is, that peace will provide the means to economic security and a livelihood. Many writers note the tendencies for an economy of war and violence to thrive during the chaos of civil war and for ex-combatants to continue to make their economic livelihoods through banditry after the war is over. To convince people to give up their guns is to convince them that there are alternative ways to earn a living. There is a need for development and economic growth to occur to extend the time horizons of disadvantaged groups in society and to deter them from contemplating a return to violence. A long time horizon requires predictability and security of investments in social, human and economic capital.

The imperatives of disarmament, de-mining and the effective demobilization of troops are obvious. The reconstruction of basic infrastructure, such as transportation and communications, is essential. The reconstruction of social infrastructure is also necessary, with education and health being foremost. Alleviating the plight of the dislocated, protecting

them from threats, providing access to land and basic tools are all critical
economic security-building measures.

Conclusion

Lack of precision and clarity of goals at the early stages of negotiation and
mediation contributes substantially to the collapse of agreements during the
implementation phase. To be sure, where a firm basis for a peaceful
relationship between warring parties is lacking, a degree of ambiguity may
be necessary to gain the consent of the adversaries to an accord. However,
the price of such ambiguity may prove extremely high. It is not enough to
bring about a handshake between adversaries; rather, peace is furthered
where the parties have carefully negotiated their differences and accepted
the new rules of competition. It is unrealistic to expect short cuts to secure
a quick and easy transition from civil war to normal relations.

Co-ordination among global, regional, state and non-state actors is
crucial in implementing peace agreements and promoting a return to normal
relations. The costs of demobilization and the reintegration of the armed
forces, if properly implemented, are extremely high, but critical, as are
security-building measures among war-weary publics. The reconstruction
of the economic and social infrastructure and the resumption of economic
activity after a civil war are central tasks in a peace-building environment.
Exhausted states cannot accomplish more than a minimum on their own and
therefore require substantial assistance during and, as importantly, *after* the
transition period.

NOTES

1. Alan James, 'Peacekeeping in the Post-Cold War Era', *International Journal*, Vol.1, No.2,
   1995, p.262. James is only partly correct about civil wars: in the twentieth century only about
   15 per cent of them have ended through a negotiated settlement. The corresponding figure
   for inter-state wars is about 50 per cent. See Stephen John Stedman, 'Negotiation and
   Mediation in Internal Conflicts', in Michael E. Brown (ed.), *The International Dimensions
   of Internal Conflicts*, Cambridge: MIT Press, 1996, pp.341–76.
2. David Rieff, 'The UN and Bosnia: the Institution that Saw No Evil', *New Republic*, Vol.214,
   No.7, 1996.
3. Stephen John Stedman, 'UN Intervention in Civil Wars: Imperatives of Choice and Strategy',
   in Donald C.F. Daniel and Bradd C. Hayes (eds.), *Beyond Traditional Peacekeeping*,
   London: Macmillan, 1995, pp.40–60; and Stedman, 'Consent, Neutrality, and Impartiality in
   the Tower of Babel: UN Peacekeeping in the 1990s', UN Institute for Disarmament Research
   paper, Geneva, 1996.
4. Eva Bertram, 'Reinventing Governments: the Promise and Perils of United Nations
   Peacebuilding', *Journal of Conflict Resolution*, Vol.39, No.3, 1995, pp.387–418.
5. See Roy Licklider, 'The Consequences of Negotiated Settlements in Civil Wars,
   1945–1993', *American Political Science Review*, Vol. 89, No.3, 1995, pp.681–90; Harrison
   Wagner, 'The Causes of Peace', in Licklider (ed.), *Stopping the Killing: How Civil Wars End*,

New York: New York University Press, 1993, pp.235–68; and Edward E. Azar, 'Protracted International Conflicts: Ten Propositions', in Azar and John W. Burton (eds.), *International Conflict Resolution*, Brighton: Wheatsheaf, 1986, pp.28ff.

6. See Alvaro de Soto and Graciana del Castillo, 'Obstacles to Peacebuilding,' *Foreign Policy*, No.94, 1994, pp.69–83; Stedman (n.1); and Susan Willett, 'Ostriches, Wise Old Elephants and Economic Reconstruction in Mozambique', *International Peacekeeping*, Vol.2, No.1, 1995, pp.34–55.

7. Adam Przeworski, *Democracy and the Market*, Cambridge: Cambridge University Press, 1991, p.26.

8. Johan Jorgen Holst, 'Confidence-building Measures: a Conceptual Framework', *Survival*, Vol.25, No.1, 1983.

9. On bargaining as an extended learning process in the African context, see Donald Rothchild, *Racial Bargaining in Independent Kenya*, London: Oxford University Press, 1973, pp.13, 145.

10. This section is an adapted and revised version of Stedman (n.1), pp.363–74.

11. See Barbara F. Walter, 'The Resolution of Civil Wars: Why Negotiations Fail', PhD thesis, University of Chicago, Dec. 1994. On the problem of commitment, see James D. Fearon, 'Commitment Problems and the Spread of Ethnic Conflict', paper delivered at the University of California, Institute on Global Conflict and Co-operation Project on the International Spread and Management of Ethnic Conflict, Palm Desert, Nov. 1995.

12. Michael Doyle, *UN Peacekeeping in Cambodia: UNTAC's Civil Mandate*, International Peace Academy Occasional Paper Series, Boulder, CO: Lynne Rienner, 1995, p.82.

13. Trevor Findlay, *Cambodia: the Legacy and Lessons of UNTAC*, Oxford: Oxford University Press for SIPRI, Research Report No.9, 1995, p.135.

14. Steven R. Ratner, *The New UN Peacekeeping: Building Peace in Lands of Conflict after the Cold War*, New York: St. Martin's Press, 1995, pp.211–12. US policy-makers at the Pentagon have expressed a similar sentiment regarding American willingness to support particular UN peace missions. According to one, US doubts about the will of Rwandans to make peace led to lukewarm American support for a peacekeeping mission to implement the Arusha Accords and contributed to delays in discussing and voting on the mission at the SC (confidential interview). For a further discussion of the difficulties in judging the sincerity of parties who sign peace accords in civil war, see Stedman, 'UN Intervention' (n.3), pp.56–7.

15. Ratner, for example, characterizes the peace settlement in Namibia as one: 'negotiated directly by all the parties representing effective sources of power in the conflict, out of a genuine spirit of reconciliation'; Ratner (n.14), p.29. In fact, while the South West African People's Organization (SWAPO), Namibia's main nationalist party, negotiated over terms of independence in the late 1970s and early 1980s, it was omitted from the four-party talks in 1988 between South Africa, Angola, Cuba and the US that led directly to the Namibian settlement. The end of the war was a period of great suspicion between the former warring parties.

16. Virginia Page Fortna, 'Success and Failure in Southern Africa: Peacekeeping in Namibia and Angola', in Daniel and Hayes (n.3), p.283.

17. The word 'guarantee' should be dropped from the mediation/implementation lexicon. The provision of guarantees by third parties suggests that the parties to a conflict can act without risk; that if their opponent acts in bad faith, they will be protected. Although third-party interventions may reduce risk and bolster the confidence of disputants, they do not guarantee that the parties will fulfil their obligations.

18. As Gordon Craig and Alexander George suggest, coercive diplomacy is more likely to succeed when the magnitude of the demands asked of the target is small. See their discussion of this point with regard to Bosnia in Craig and George, *Force and Statecraft*, New York: Oxford University Press, 3rd edn, 1995, pp.271–2.

19. 'Cambodia: Human Rights before and after the Elections', *Asia Watch*, Vol.5, No.10, 1993, p.7; cited in Findlay (n.13), p.129.

20. Findlay (n.13), p.129.

21. Ibid., pp.131–2.

22. Doyle (n.12), p.82.

23. Ratner (n.14), pp.200–2.
24 Confidential interview.
25. Ibid.
26. Ratner (n.14), p.50.
27. See Peter Batchelor, 'Disarmament, Small Arms and Internal Conflict: the Case of Southern Africa'; and Chris Smith, 'Light Weapons, Peacekeeping, Disarmament and Security: a Case Study of Southern Africa', Geneva: UN Institute for Disarmament Research, Project on Disarmament and Conflict Resolution, policy papers, 1996.
28. Findlay (n.13), pp.113–16; and Doyle (n.12), p.83.
29. De Soto and del Castillo (n.6), pp.69–83.
30. Ibid., p.71; and Willet (n.6).
31. *Economist*, 28 Oct. 1995, p.46.
32. William Shawcross, *Cambodia's New Deal*, Contemporary Issues Paper No.1, Washington, DC: Carnegie Endowment for International Peace, 1994, pp.87–8.
33. Gobierno de El Salvador, *Avance de los Programs de Reinsercion*, San Salvador: Secretaria de Reconstruccion Nacional, Feb. 1995, p.5. The authors thank Lael Parish for obtaining and translating this and other documents from El Salvador.
34. Findlay (n.13), p.169.
35. See, for example, the recommendations of Jarat Chopra, 'Back to the Drawing Board', *Bulletin of the Atomic Scientists*, Mar./Apr. 1995, pp.29–35.
36. James Macintosh, 'Confidence-building Measures – a Conceptual Exploration', in R.B. Byers, F. Stephen Larrabee and Allen Lynch (eds.), *Confidence-building Measures and International Security*, New York: Institute for East-West Security Studies, 1987, p.16.
37. Ibid., pp.16–18.
38. James A. Schear, 'Verification, Compliance and Arms Control: the Dynamics of Domestic Debate', in Lynn Eden and Steven E. Miller (eds.), *Nuclear Arguments: Understanding the Strategic Nuclear Arms and Arms Control Debates*, Ithaca, NY: Cornell, 1989, p.265.
39. Ibid., p.268.
40. Ibid., p.266.
41. Ibid.
42. Craig D. Parks, Robert Henager and Shawn Scamahorn, 'Trust and Reactions to Messages of Intent in Social Dilemmas', *Journal of Conflict Resolution*, Vol.40, No.1, 1996, pp.134–51.
43. The following three paragraphs are adapted from Donald Rothchild, 'On Implementing Africa's Peace Accords: from Defection to Co-operation', *Africa Today*, Vol.42, Nos.1–2, 1995, pp.15–16, 31.
44. See Iraê Baptista Lundin, 'Cultural Diversity and the Role of Traditional Authority in Mozambique', in Donald Rothchild (ed.), *Strengthening African Local Initiative: Local Self-Governance, Decentralisation and Accountability*, Hamburg: Africa Institute, 1994, Ch.8.
45. Republic of Mozambique, *General Peace Agreement of Mozambique 1992*, p.54.
46. Republic of South Africa, 'Constitution of the Republic of South Africa', 1993, *Government Gazette*, 343, 15466, 28 Jan. 1994, Ch.1.

Beyond Post-Conflict Peacebuilding: What Links to Sustainable Development and Human Security?

TIMOTHY M. SHAW

The proliferation of peacekeeping and coalition operations in Africa over the last five to ten years poses profound challenges for analysis and praxis, explanation and prescription. This article is premised on the assumption that at least some of the causes of the social conflicts – that have led to the growing demand for diverse elements in the peacekeeping nexus – lie in the character and consequences of structural adjustment programmes. The seeming elusiveness of sustainable development and human security in Africa raises questions about prospects for the consolidation of either capitalism or democracy. Rather, varieties of corporatism, authoritarianism and anarchy are more likely to emerge in the next century. The central role of civil society – at local, national, regional and global levels – is crucial in determining which scenario is most plausible, given the heterogeneity in Africa's political economies and cultures. Hence the imperative of including civil society in any analytic and prescriptive purview of structural adjustment and peacekeeping.

> West Africa is becoming *the* symbol of worldwide demographic, environmental, and social stress, in which criminal anarchy emerges as the real 'strategic' danger.[1]

Africa: from Neo-Liberal Reforms to Peacekeeping Operations

This article seeks to situate the emerging discourses about the peacekeeping nexus in Africa and elsewhere in the contexts of new international divisions of labour (NIDL) and power (NIDP) in the post-bipolar world. In particular, it seeks to probe the connection between ubiquitous structural adjustment programmes (SAPs) and the emergence of numerous complex emergencies. These, in fact, may not be 'emergencies' at all, but rather the predictable, structural consequences of the profound economic contractions which have resulted from the reforms insisted upon by the international financial institutions (IFIs). Indeed, the interrelated costs of both SAPs and emergencies are indicative not only of the problems of effecting neo-liberal

Timothy M. Shaw is Professor of Political Science and International Development Studies and Director of the Centre for Foreign Policy Studies at Dalhousie University.

reforms on the African continent and elsewhere, but also of the elusiveness of human development and security. As the United Nations Development Programme (UNDP) notes:

> The concept of human development is much broader than the conventional theories of economic development...It analyses all issues in society – whether economic growth, trade, employment, political freedom or cultural values – from the perspective of people. It thus focuses on enlarging human choices...There are four major elements in the concept of human development:...productivity, equity, sustainability and empowerment.[2]

In short, the hypothesis advanced here is that the marginalization of many African communities and countries in an era characterized by neo-liberal hegemony and exponential globalization has generated the conditions which call for multi-faceted peacekeeping coalitions, if even minimal levels of stability and security are to be regained. So it is suggested that it is not coincidental that Africa is economically marginal, yet central to the peacekeeping nexus – the need for the latter is embedded in the former. Unless SAP terms are modified and moderated before the end of this century, Africa's economic marginalization and peacekeeping proliferation is likely to continue well into the next.[3]

Meanwhile, the political economy/culture of most of Africa is quite transformed as we approach the next millennium. The combined and cumulative impacts of 15 years of structural adjustment conditionalities and five years of the post-Cold War era and, happily, of the ending of apartheid, have led to both marginalization and re-evaluation. Unhappily, much analysis on and about Africa has been less than realistic or responsive, reinforcing inappropriate perspectives and policies. While we may all concur with Maynes's lament that, 'The problem is Sub-Saharan Africa',[4] we do not have to accept Kaplan's all-too-influential 1994 apocalyptic visions of either West Africa or an anarchic world.[5]

Nevertheless, such formulations do have important implications for both conventional and unconventional security dilemmas and debates with respect to Africa.[6] In part, in addition to suggesting shifts in the context and the conceptual approach, this revisionist perspective seeks to juxtapose several fields of analysis not often associated in Africa or elsewhere. This is necessitated, it is argued, by the explanatory, let alone prescriptive, challenges posed by contemporary Africa. In particular, in an appropriately modified critical form, the following conceptual perspectives can contribute to an understanding of the continent's current unenviable condition:[7]

• comparative politics/political economy, with a focus on redefined states, economies and societies which have undergone SAPs and formal liberalization leading towards multiparty constitutions and elections;

- international relations/foreign policy, particularly when refocused to treat 'new' issues such as debt, drugs, the environment, ethnicity and informal sectors, and non-state actors, such as non-governmental organizations (NGOs) and multinational corporations, as well as states;

- international and regional organizations/human rights/civil society, such as the UN, the Organization for African Unity (OAU), the Economic Community of West African States (ECOWAS), the Inter-Governmental Authority on Drought and Development (IGADD) and the Southern African Development Community (SADC). Also, more informal groupings of presidents, civil societies and their legal superstructures, including human rights, democratic development declarations and agreements;

- the area of development studies, with its concentration not only on policies and projects, but also constraints, traditions and sustainability. Development studies now constitutes a field which extends to human development within communities and regions, as well as countries or states;

- human security studies, which is redirecting strategic studies away from bipolar, nuclear, orthodox state-centric concerns towards a focus on community, development, economics, the environment, gender issues; and,

- peacekeeping studies, which is blossoming into a distinctive sub-field of its own, building on previous short-term humanitarian, disaster, negotiation and reconstruction concerns, to include longer-term peacekeeping 'interventions',[8] encompassing the spectrum from election monitoring to post-conflict rehabilitation, rather than just 'blue beret' and diplomatic functions.

There is also an intellectual-cum-political imperative to this revisionism and juxtapositioning of approaches. To date, advocates of the hegemonic, neo-liberal paradigm have successfully avoided any responsibility for either the negative social consequences of adjustment or the incidence of intense conflicts and the consequent range of peacekeeping responses. Further, the orthodox 'modernization' perspective has been rehabilitated by the 're-democracy' movement with its focus on formal multipartyism, rather than less formal civil society.

Finally, Africa's woes have been exaggerated and popularized by Kaplan and others, who decontextualize and universalize the continent's not inconsiderable difficulties. Such uncritical assertions need to be challenged by more authentic, radical and informed scholarship which puts contemporary SAPs and peacemaking in perspective. Hence the reformulations presented below.

The emerging 'discipline' of peacekeeping, or, more broadly, peace operations, is diverse in terms of activities and roles, and institutions and actors. It may be seen to encompass:

- early-warning methods and responses, particularly local, non-state, rather than global/statist entities;

- democratic development – not just formal multiparty constitutions and elections, but also local decision-making and facilitation of an increasingly heterogeneous civil society;

- confidence-building measures (CBMs), again not just between political or military parties but also within countries;

- classic peacekeeping 'interventions', if ethnic or other conflicts cannot be contained, but also advancing to peace-building and peacemaking if conditions necessitate; these interventions routinely tend to be multinational in composition and to involve non-state actors, particularly local and global NGOs; and,

- post-conflict rehabilitation and reconstruction of both state and society, economy and infrastructure, while avoiding any repetition of pre-conflict catalysts; this is a long-term process involving non-state, rather than state actors, to rebuild a resilient civil society through truly sustainable human development/security.

Africa's Fate: from Structural Adjustment to Peacebuilding?

Africa itself offers a range of cases and lessons relevant to these topologies, starting with the classic instances of the Suez Canal and Katanga in the early post-colonial independence period, to the contemporary traumas of Liberia, Somalia and Rwanda. It also illustrates the long-term legacies of Cold War and apartheid interventions in, say, the Horn of Africa (Ethiopia, Somalia and Sudan) and southern Africa, especially Angola and Mozambique, but also Zaire.

Yet the continent also indicates the proliferating incidences and profound impacts of SAPs. These have reinforced the largely negative consequences of globalization, itself advanced by the hegemony of neo-liberalism since the early 1980s. By the late 1970s, Africa was in a crisis of development, in terms of both achievements and policies, as the classic one-party or military state was clearly not delivering sustainable development. It was peculiarly vulnerable therefore to external, especially IFI, pressures to repay debts and redirect policies away from any aspirations towards 'self-reliance' and back towards external integration. It is argued here that the current imperative of the peacekeeping nexus in Africa derives from this early advocacy of SAPs, which rapidly became embedded in its political economy and culture. The costs of adjustment, then, are not only shorter-term and developmental but also longer-term strategic.

There is now a substantial literature on the causes, consequences and explanations of SAPs in Africa and elsewhere. This broadly divides neo-classical economists from more radical or sceptical social scientists. The former are best reflected in World Bank and International Bank for Reconstruction and Development (IBRD) studies from 1979 to 1984, which asserted that if official African 'reform' policies – market forces rather than state interventions – advanced devaluation, deregulation, desubsidisation, elimination of disincentives and bottlenecks, downsizing of the bureaucracy, privatization and so forth, then growth could be recaptured.[9]

Despite perpetual lacklustre performances by almost all criteria, the neo-liberals continue to assert that Africa can yet achieve some economic successes if it persists along the SAP path. By contrast, liberals are concerned about slippages, particularly the tension between economic and political liberalizations. Finally, the radicals dismiss reformist prospects, arguing that the imperative of sustainable development necessitates a rethinking of state-civil society relations, with a renewed emphasis on aspects such as education, gender, health, informal sectors, infrastructures and regionalisms.

These analytical approaches can hardly be reconciled as they reflect divergent problematiques, so the academic and policy disagreements persist. To be sure, there have been attempts to transcend these continuing stand-offs. First, in particular during the 1990s, there has been a proliferation of comparative studies, not just among African cases but also between Africa and comparable regions in the South, notably, Latin America and South Asia. Secondly, there has been a novel shift in focus to 'transitions' largely outside Africa in the former 'Second World' countries, but sometimes embracing former Soviet allies or associates in Africa, such as Angola, Ethiopia, Mozambique and Somalia. And last, there has been a growth industry concerning which lessons from the newly-industrializing countries (NICs) and near-NICs have been applied to Africa and other parts of the South undertaking SAPs. While such comparisons may provide some insights into SAP policies and consequences, they tend to be rather narrowly focused on formal economies, rather than informal political and social relations. They rarely examine issues of sustainable development, let alone prospects for complex emergencies.

In general, the results of homogeneous SAPs in Africa's heterogeneous states have been negative in terms of sustainable human development/ security, reinforcing the continent's marginalization for almost all except the IFIs and the NGOs. SAPs have contributed to:

- lacklustre economic performances in aggregate and per capita terms over the last couple of decades, so that national and personal incomes have stagnated at best, or often declined in the majority of countries;

- divergent classes, with the post-independence middle class largely disappearing and only a small minority clinging on to upper-class incomes, property and life-style; by contrast, the total and relative numbers of poor have grown dramatically, leading to brain-drains, refugees, the growth of informal sectors and crime. This has contributed to fertile grounds for ethnic, racial and religious antagonisms and fundamentalisms;

- declining standards of education, health and infrastructures as the state shrinks and 'real' budgets disappear, leading to a two-tier system of world-class private facilities for the affluent minority and international non-governmental organizations (INGOs) providing basic needs for the rest; and

- increasing levels of informal sectors, crime and insecurity, in which informal markets and employment are crucial for survival; this includes increasing gang violence and robberies, and as personal and communal insecurity mounts, the emergence of a range of private security arrangements and vigilantes.

SAP conditionalities have proliferated with the end of the Cold War away from exclusively economic imperatives towards political and social reforms, notably the democratization of formal governance, but also the reduction and capping of the military and the advancing of ecological concerns. The compatibility of such multiplying SAP terms remains even more problematic than traditional conditions, yet donors among the Organization for Economic Co-operation and Development (OECD), as well as IFIs, increasingly insist on them. Domestic pressures for political liberalization preceded SAP negotiations, in part because of internal resistance. Local demands were reinforced internationally by post-Cold War pressures for democratization.

Re-democratization of formal governance structures has not been a singular success in Africa thus far. To be sure, national conventions, constitutions and elections have been organized, leading to a few overdue changes in regimes. However, some elections have been hijacked by incumbents (Kenya) or soldiers (Niger) and some new regimes have performed little better than their predecessors (Zambia). Further, some elections were not allowed to proceed (Nigeria). Notwithstanding a few successes, such as South Africa, Malawi, Botswana and Namibia, the anticipated second wave of democratization has not been sustained.[10]

In part, such disappointments over the apparent elusiveness of re-democratization are a function of the negative consequences of SAPs, especially the socio-political 'fallacies' of adjustment. Africa's contemporary political economies are hardly conducive to formal democratic processes, given the prevalence of unemployment, informal sectors, poverty, insecurity and low levels of Basic Human Needs (BHNs) and Human Development Indicators (HDIs). Indeed, formal multiparty constitutions and elections may revive ethnic identities and competitiveness.

Africa: Beyond Liberalization to Civil Society

Arguably, more significant and sustainable than democracy, at the formal level, is the revival of civil society, notably NGOs, but also co-operatives, religious organizations, women's movements, green groups and, especially, the media. The last have benefited from global technological and attitudinal changes. Even if it was still acceptable in practice, it is increasingly difficult for isolationist or xenophobic regimes to stop satellite television, faxes and e-mail, let alone global radio and portable telephones. Africa's new media publish in both print – business papers and news magazines – and electronically through CNN and BBC World News and private South African cable channels. The burgeoning media have advanced civil society, democracy and alternative viewpoints on issues such as corruption, democratization and privatization. But their sustainability is still problematic given hostile regimes, shrinking middle classes and regional and global competition. Yet they remain a powerful ally, as well as potential destabilizer, for any peace-building measures.

Civil society has also developed over the last decade because of demand. This demand is of three types. First, SAP reforms have reduced state welfare and have led to alternative providers of education, health and other basic needs, notably local and global NGOs. Secondly, IFIs have increasingly subcontracted programmes and projects to INGOs and NGOs, leading to the difficult dilemma of co-optation. And thirdly, some local and global NGOs have become important players, especially serving as adjuncts to blue berets in terms of refugee support, small-scale employment and repatriations. In short, INGOs and NGOs have become increasingly important in Africa's political economy and culture. For INGOs and NGOs, Africa is central not marginal:

> The notion of Africa's marginalization, while stemming from the concrete reality of super-power disengagement, is facile...a variety of NGOs have directed international concern to sub-Saharan Africa.[11]

The emerging peacekeeping literature and debates on NGOs and blue berets is welcome. There is a range of NGO-peacekeeper relationships encompassing pre- to post-conflict situations. A range of cultures are involved, complicating communications and operations. However, socialization through joint training and combined operations may enhance and sustain co-operation. Likewise, imposing practices of accountability, transparency and such like within the NGO-peacekeeping coalition should enhance confidence and predictability. NGOs will be more dominant in both the pre- and post-conflict stages, where 'subcontracting' by the UN and other agencies tends to be most frequent.[12]

If two poles of the peacekeeping syndrome are to be advanced – elections and reconstruction – and the unattractive features of the middle ground avoided, such as 'active' peacekeeping and peacemaking, then governance concerns must be integrated into operations. There are certainly complexities associated with the contemporary peacekeeping nexus and considerable challenges entailed in undertaking peacekeeping operations in chaotic and unstable theatres:

> This calls for a co-ordinated approach to peacekeeping in the NGO community. There are currently three major shortcomings. These are, respectively, insufficient upfront funding, insufficient rapid deployment capability, and insufficient inter-agency co-ordination.[13]

How the good governance mix of accountability, participation, predictability and transparency may be advanced at the fringes, as well as at the core, of the peacekeeping nexus is problematic. Continuous attention to governance is clearly vital. Relations among peacekeepers on the one hand, and regimes, economies, societies and regional structures, on the other, are crucial to any successful operational outcome. Likewise, recognition of the range of intricate governance issues within peacekeeping coalitions is imperative, if peace-building and peacemaking challenges are to be addressed successfully. If elements of good governance are internalized during periods of peacekeeping then they may be more readily effected in the delicate post-operations period.

In short, socialization during active peacekeeping conditions may subsequently advance sustainable development, so enhancing the prospects for human security and development over the longer term and minimizing those for a retreat towards instability. Happily, Africa's own institutional capacity relevant to the peacekeeping nexus has increased somewhat in recent years. The OAU under Salim Salim's energetic and innovative leadership has moved to transcend its state-centric legacy and to question the inviolability of inherited colonial borders. In addition to more open treatment of democracy and human rights issues, it has begun to establish its own Conflict Prevention and Management Mechanism. This includes a Conflict Management Centre and early warning system, and the fostering of CBMs and rapid deployment capabilities – the latter in co-operation with the European Union (EU), especially France and Britain. As Maynes notes:

> the world needs a plan for Africa. We may need to go back to square one, offering aid to Africans in a regional context, perhaps even providing incentives to redraw borders to obtain more viable states. We should be willing to adopt the French idea of an intra-African legion so that order can be restored to areas subject to ethnic violence.[14]

Africa's New Security Challenges and Constraints

Africa's NGO community has benefited from the 'liberation' and redirection of some South African institutions. In association with established pan-African groups, such as the African Centre for Development and Strategic Studies (ACDESS), the Forum of African Voluntary Development Organizations (FAVDO), MWENGO, the African Centre for the Constructive Resolution of Disputes (ACCORD), the Centre for Conflict Resolution (CCR) and the Institute for Defence Policy (IDP), NGOs have begun to provide a non-official capacity for more independent research and advice, as in the remodelled SADC. Nathan provides an informed overview of the post-apartheid evolution of, and debates about, southern Africa's new security architecture, which transcends established state-centrism:

> A broad consensus has emerged around the following themes: new thinking on security; common secularity; disarmament; and peaceful resolution of conflict.[15]

The continent's NGOs have been able to begin to match extra-continental inputs to the development of peacekeeping policy and practice. It is to be hoped that the novel OAU mechanism will be able to work with the emerging African NGO network over redefinitions of security, peace-building, CBMs and reconstruction. Any such sustainable arrangements would include the ensuring that authentic regional issues are on the global agenda, such as the plague of small arms – especially the flood of AK47 assault rifles and landmines – indigenous notions of peacemaking, gender and the environment.

Jacklyn Cock provides a disturbingly comprehensive view of one distinctive aspect of current security issues that has profound and negative consequences for effective peace-building: the proliferation of, trade in and use of these light weapons.[16] She identifies the broad range of state and non-state actors who exploit their access to these efficient, destructive weapons, from political extremists, mercenaries, poachers and criminals to private security firms and vigilantes. The sequence of destabilization and demobilization, under situations of economic and ecological crisis, have encouraged resort to AK47s, exacerbated by active demand and trade across borders. Any long-term resolution of conflict throughout the region will require simultaneous improvements of an economic, strategic, political and environmental nature, involving both state and non-state organizations in CBMs and peace-building. Sustainable development is clearly problematic with so many landmines in the fields and roads and AK47s in the hands and houses of people in Africa. Yet global negotiations to contain, or outlaw, the use and production of small arms are being slowed down, as the relatively powerless see them as essential elements in their armouries. Meanwhile, NGOs are involved in a range of direct activities to identify, disarm and recycle such weapons, especially landmines. They are also associated with the depressing, yet essential, task of procuring and fitting prosthetics for Africa's maimed generation.

Africa may yet be able to orchestrate at both the regional and the continental level a set of 'track two'-type arrangements, which would parallel those in the Asia-Pacific region:[17] rounds of unofficial, yet also well-connected discussions about functional or technical CBMs. In dramatically different circumstances, Africa may yet be able to advance preventive or precautionary conflict-avoidance, as well as peace-building activities, for the next millennium. Already the talks about an Association of Southern African States (ASAS), based on CCR, and other inputs, are not so dissimilar from the role which the ASEAN – ISIS (Association of South-East Asian Studies – Institutes for Strategic and International Studies) and the Council for Security Co-operation in Asia Pacific (CSCAP) play in south-east Asia, particularly over the South China Sea imbroglio, but also over coastal zone management, piracy, rescue at sea and shipping lanes. CCR and others have suggested a range of pan-African socialization measures, including regular meetings among the continent's Chiefs of Staff, a peacekeeping contact group and a Pan-African Staff College. However, Marstein has cautioned about unrealistic regional expectations concerning post-apartheid South Africa's state and non-state leadership roles and resources in terms of the peacekeeping nexus:

These expectations, however, entail unrealistic expectations of South Africa's financial capabilities, and are mixed with a fear of a new South African hegemony.[18]

Among the complicating inheritances of the peacekeeping nexus is the continuing ambiguity over the place of post-independence militaries in African states. The ambiguity continues despite the end of both the Cold War and the apartheid system and the reappearance of coups and praetorian regimes in the mid 1990s. Indeed, if anything, the relationship between militaries, the police and the intelligence services, and the supposedly civilian regimes is even more problematic in the SAP period, with formal democratization contrasting with army involvements and even interventions. In reality, vulnerable leaders rely more on coercion and corporatism than co-optation and corruption. Yet the dynamism of civil society may somewhat moderate and mitigate such regressive tendencies, especially given the NGOs' set of connections with the peacekeeping coalition.

However, whether the present with its SAPs will facilitate containment of the security forces – no longer just the diverse range of official organizations, but now extending to semi-private security organizations and vigilantes – remains problematic. But at least these longstanding issues should now be placed on the agenda of sustainable/human development, particularly in terms of the emerging peacekeeping nexus. We should retain some objectivity and scepticism lest the peacemaking syndrome becomes merely a legitimation for a remodelled military-industrial complex.

Already some established military leaders in and outside Africa seek to retain, or regain, legitimacy, revenues, technologies and resources through peacekeeping roles – either operational or stand-by – so resisting SAP terms of a two per cent cap on any state's military expenditures. Just as the military was seen within the prevailing modernization paradigm to be vital for security in the South in the post-independence, bipolar era, so SAP stability may be advanced by reference to blue berets. Novel forms of post-conflict corporatism might be anticipated, in which 'successful' peacekeepers play a major praetorian role in a wide range of contexts, including CBMs. In short, peacekeeping corporatism may come to advance established interests in a post-conflict situation, serving to rehabilitate militaristic responses and expenditures.

Peacekeeping in Africa may also involve mercenary as well as militaristic elements. First, state militaries may seek not only to enhance their status through peacekeeping but also to augment their foreign exchange incomes by supplying troops at the relatively advantageous UN US dollar rate, so making at least a part of their corporate income separate from the SAP-supervised national accounts. Moreover, some developing world regimes may be quite accustomed to supplementing their minimal incomes through informal trade, including coercive 'rent' collecting; such customary practices may undermine peacekeeping's effectiveness, let alone its image.

Secondly, both states and civil societies may seek protection during complex emergencies through the hiring of informal mercenary soldiers. Such mercenaries may, of course, be ex- or part-time soldiers, or operatives in informal sectors. In any event, further privatization of security in Africa, no matter how good the intentions, poses problems for sustainable development in the future.

Africa's Futures and Peacemaking Coalitions

In conclusion, five distinct scenarios may be abstracted, relating to Africa's political economy, globalization and SAP conditionalities, and the peacekeeping nexus, namely:

- a scenario of SAP success leading to economic rejuvenation which would, in theory, trickle down, in turn minimizing inequalities and those factors which cause conflicts, and stimulate peacekeeping responses;

- partial, but uneven, results from SAPs leading to unpredictable demands for peacekeeping, ranging from electoral monitoring to short-term peacemaking, but not longer-term rehabilitation;

- a divergence between Third, Fourth and Fifth World[19] states, in which the latter would need continual peace-building attention, which some of the former would begin to be in a position to provide themselves;

- a divergence between regions in which the poorer require more peacekeeping responses and resources than the richer; and

- a doomsday scenario of anarchy as predicted by Kaplan, in which peacekeeping responses are required to keep even minimal levels of stability and which would exercise the full range of responses, from CBMs to reconstruction.

To be sure, some combination or sequence of these five is most likely at the turn of the new century; these would, one would hope, encompass the fourth scenario back to the first – should the NIDL and NIDP prove conducive – or, vice versa if the peacekeeping coalition is not efficacious. In any event, in the interrelated SAP and peacekeeping discourses, even if not in the global political economy itself, Africa will be central. As Pliny the Elder proverbially cautioned nearly two millennia ago, *ex Africa, semper aliquid novi*. Similarly, in its latest global report *The World in 1996*, *The Economist* cautions about, 'a dangerous century ahead'.[20]

NOTES

1. Robert Kaplan, 'The Coming Anarchy', *Atlantic Monthly*, Vol.273, No.2, Feb. 1994, p.46.
2. UNDP, *Human Development Report 1995*, New York: Oxford University Press, 1995, pp.ll–12.
3. See Timothy M. Shaw, 'Africa within the New World Order: Marginal and/or Central?', in Adebayo Adedeji (ed.), *Africa within the World: beyond Dispossession and Dependence*, London: Zed Press for ACDESS, 1993, pp.78–93.
4. Charles William Maynes, 'The New Pessimism', *Foreign Policy*, No.100, Fall 1995, p.48.
5. See Kaplan, (n.1), pp.44–75.
6. See Timothy M. Shaw and Clement E. Adibe, 'Africa and Global Developments in the Twenty-first Century', *International Journal*, Vol.51, No.1, Winter 1995–96, pp.1–26.
7. See Timothy M. Shaw, 'Africa in the Global Political Economy at the End of the Millennium: what Implications for Politics and Policies?', *Africa Today*, Vol.42, No.4, 1995, pp.7–30.
8. See Stephen John Stedman, 'The New Interventionists', *Foreign Affairs*, Vol.72, No.1, 1993, pp.1–16.
9. See Adedeji (ed.), *Africa within the World*; Michael Barratt Brown, *Africa's Choices: After Thirty Years of the World Bank*, Harmondsworth: Penguin, 1995; and Giovanni Andrea Cornia, Rolph van der Hoeven and Thandika Mkandawire (eds.), *Africa Recovery in the 1990s: from Stagnation and Adjustment to Development*, London: Macmillan for UNICEF, 1992.
10. See I. William Zartman (ed.), *Collapsed States: the Disintegration and Restoration of Legitimate Authority*, Boulder, CO: Lynne Rienner, 1995.
11. Special Issue on Sub-Saharan Africa, *Journal of International Affairs*, Vol.46, No.1, Summer 1992, p.1.
12. See Thomas G. Weiss and Edwin S. Smith (eds.), *UN Subcontracting for Security and Services: Burden-sharing with Regional and Non-governmental Organizations*, London: Macmillan 1997 for ACUNS, forthcoming.
13. Sigurd Marstein, 'NGOs in Peacekeeping Operations', *African Security Review*, Vol.4, No.6, 1995, pp.6–7.
14. Maynes (n.4), p.48.
15. Laurie Nathan, 'Formalising Conflict Resolution and Security Arrangements in Southern Africa', Johannesburg: ACDESS, Jan. 1996, p.3.
16. See Jacklyn Cock, 'The Link between Security and Development: the Problem of Light Weapons Proliferation in Southern Africa', Johannesburg: ACDESS, Jan. 1996.
17. See Paul T. Mitchell, Fahimul Quadir, Timothy M. Shaw and Janis van der Westhuizen, 'Prospects for a New Political Economy of Development and Security in the Twenty-first Century: Comparative Insights', Toronto: CANCAPS, Apr. 1996.
18. Marstein, (n.13), p.14. See also Janis van der Westhuizen, 'Can the Giant Be Gentle? Peace-making as South African Foreign Policy', *Politikon*, Vol.22, No.2, Dec. 1995, pp.72–85.
19. Less Developed (LDC), Least Developed (LLDC) and Failed Countries.
20. *The Economist*, *The World in 1996*, London: Economist Intelligence Unit, 1995, p.13.

OPERATIONAL ISSUES AND CASE STUDIES:
AFRICA FOCUS

The Issue of the Military: UN Demobilization, Disarmament and Reintegration in Southern Africa

CHRIS ALDEN

This article will analyse the United Nations' experience of demilitarization in southern Africa with reference to peacekeeping missions and the transition from emergency to developmental contexts. Three UN peace-support operations in southern Africa – the UN Transition Assistance Group (UNTAG), the UN Operation in Mozambique (ONUMOZ) and the UN Angola Verification Mission (UNAVEM) – will be examined to assess the international organization's role. The article focuses on the importance of developing a regional approach to demilitarization; the imperative of co-operation both within the UN itself and the international donor and non-governmental organization (NGO) community as a whole; and the need to develop a greater understanding of the efficacy of 'targeting' demilitarization programmes towards ex-combatants.

The demilitarization of combatants – a process which encompasses the demobilization and disarmament of troops and their reintegration into society[1] – has as its premise the proposition that combatants are particularly dangerous elements to interject into a fluid post-conflict situation. Both the perpetrators and, as often, the objects of brutalizing violence, combatants have the capacity to disrupt the fragile peace settlement, either by returning to open hostilities with their opponents or resorting to armed banditry in the aftermath of a formal declaration of peace. Accordingly, it has become a kind of cardinal principle that this volatility may be offset through a targeted programme which builds on the structured demobilization and disarmament of combatants, in conjunction with monetary and educational incentives designed to facilitate the peaceful reintroduction of combatants into civilian life. This two-phased approach to the question of demilitarization is composed of both the short-term objectives of emergency assistance and the long-term objectives of development. As such, it is subject to all of the complexities inherent in the emergency to relief continuum.

The demilitarization programmes instituted by the UN have, in the main, recognized the necessity of extending the scope of demilitarization beyond the short-term objectives of demobilization and disarmament. In the lexicon

Chris Alden is a lecturer in International Relations in the University of Witwatersrand, South Africa.

of the UN, peace-building represents the transitional point between the demobilization of combatants and their full reintegration into society:

> Peacemaking and peacekeeping operations, to be truly successful, must come to include comprehensive efforts to identify and support structures which will tend to consolidate peace...[T]he concept of peace-building as the construction of a new environment should be viewed as a counterpart of preventive diplomacy.[2]

Nevertheless, conceptual clarity is needed if UN peace support operations are to act effectively in this area. In the same vein, it is noted that the controversies which often attend project design and implementation in demilitarization are themselves a product of this disjuncture between the emergency ethos and the development ethos.[3] Indeed, it is the contention of one Special Representative of the Secretary-General (SRSG) that this disjuncture is one of the major failings of UN peace-support operations.[4] The gap between the emergency and development is more than a mere intellectual oversight to be recognized and corrected; it finds institutional expression in the plethora of UN agencies which make up such operations.

A further complication is the role of the international NGO community, which itself is divided along the emergency and development fault line and, accordingly, acts with varying degrees of autonomy from UN peace-support operations. This has the effect, at times, of contradicting the aims of the mission and, in other instances, ameliorating the failings of the UN.

The UN, Demilitarization and the Southern African Context

Demilitarization, as it has become abundantly clear in the wake of UN involvement in southern Africa, is not a national problem but rather a regional one. The three cases from southern Africa – Namibia, Angola and Mozambique – provide valuable examples of UN involvement in demilitarization, highlighting the strengths and weaknesses of its changing approach in the region. Most notably, the UN refined its demilitarization programme to include both short- and long-term components, as well as moving towards an integrated and comprehensive approach to the issue of the military. In each case study the following areas will be examined: the demilitarization programme as conceived in the peace settlement; the demilitarization programme as organized by the UN peace-support operation; and the record of implementation.

Namibia and UNTAG

Established in the wake of the signing of the New York Accords in

December 1988, Namibia was the first post-Cold War mission of the UN, the largest peacekeeping operation since the ill-fated mission to the Congo and the most complex undertaken by the organization at the time. As such, it posed a series of challenges to the UN's capacity to conduct a multi-dimensional operation that incorporated elements of traditional peacekeeping as well as novel components in such areas as policing and election monitoring. Its successful conclusion, despite some serious incidents, gave considerable encouragement to the international community as to the efficacy of extending the UN role in peacekeeping world-wide.

The Peace Agreement and Demilitarization

The agreement formally ending the conflict in Namibia had in fact been drawn up in 1978 under the auspices of the UN's Western Contact Group. Security Council Resolution (SCR) 435 (1978), which called for the withdrawal of the South African military, administrative control over the territory and democratic elections, and formed the basis for the cessation of hostilities and the transition to independence. Following the assent of all parties to the New York Accords, the Security Council (SC) passed Resolution 629 (1989), which officially established the Namibian mission. Accordingly, the UN was charged with the supervision of the cease-fire, the monitoring of the conduct of the South West African Police (SWAPOL) and observing the election campaign. The timetable for the operation was to cover 12 months and involved the following steps:

- a cease-fire was to be formally established on 1 April;

- the disbanding of the South West African Territorial Force (SWATF) and SWAPO and the reduction of the South African Defence Force (SADF) from 32,000 to zero by 8 November 1989;

- elections were to be held on 16 November 1989.

All of these steps were to take place in tandem with the Cuban withdrawal from Angola, overseen by UNAVEM I (see below). Overseeing the implementation of the entire process would be a SRSG and a South African-appointed Administrator-General. To fulfil the stated aims of SCR 435, UNTAG would be structured to include civil, police and military components. The civil component consisted of the SRSG's Office – which was supported by 42 smaller political offices established across Namibia's ten regions – and which would provide general direction and co-ordination to the mission, as well as preparing the foundation for UN Development Programme (UNDP) involvement after the mission. In addition, an independent jurist would arbitrate on matters relevant to the peace process; the UN High Commissioner for Refugees (UNHCR) would be responsible for the repatriation of refugees in advance of the elections; an electoral division would oversee voter registration and monitor the elections in November 1989; and there would be a logistics division. The police and the military component are discussed below.

UNTAG and Demilitarization

In the Namibian case, the UN mission's involvement in demilitarization was conceived wholly in terms of short-term objectives, that is, the demobilization and disarmament of combatants. No provisions for the reintegration of former soldiers were introduced into the programme; nor were they the recipients of any targeted projects, assistance or funding beyond that provided in the course of their stay in the reception areas. The first aspect of UNTAG's role in demilitarization centred around the supervision of the confinement, then withdrawal, of South African troops from Namibian territory, and the concomitant repatriation of SWAPO guerrillas from their bases in southern Angola and Zambia. Linked to this was the monitoring of the cease-fire between the former foes. To fulfil these objectives UNTAG was to bring in a team of 200 military observers and 7,500 peacekeepers. Their tasks were to monitor the following:

- the restriction of the SADF to bases within Namibia by 1 April 1989, and their subsequent withdrawal from the territory, with: the first reduction to 12,000 troops by 14 May 1989; to 1,500 by 1 July 1989; and total withdrawal by 8 November 1989;

- the dismantling of the SWATF, commando and ethnic units, and their disarmament by 1 April 1989;

- the disarming and repatriation of SWAPO forces, including the confining of selected forces to bases in Angola and Zambia;[5]

- the policing of official entry points into the country and reception areas for returnees.

The second aspect of UNTAG's role in demilitarization was the monitoring of the Namibian police and those elements of the SADF which had taken up civil functions during the transition period. Complicating the situation further was the incorporation of the notorious counter-insurgency unit, Koevoet, into SWAPOL. With SWAPOL given the principal role in maintaining law and order during the transitional period, it would be the job of the UN's 360-strong civil police force to ensure that it did not engage in acts of intimidation against the population during the run-up to the election. The use of civil police in fulfilling this task was one of UNTAG's innovations; no other mission had undertaken such a direct and extensive policing role.

Implementation

The implementation of the demilitarization programme was subject to the problems and constraints facing UNTAG. Despite having literally years to prepare for the mission, when it came to implementing the objectives of SCR 435(1978) it was clear that little work had been done in terms of the actual mechanics of the operation. In the first instance, delays in the passing of enabling legislation by both the SC, which authorized the particulars of the operation only on 16 February and the General Assembly (GA), which gave its approval two weeks later, cut an already narrow margin for the deployment of UNTAG to the bare minimum. With the budgetary constraints imposed by the SC, the UNTAG peacekeeping deployment was reduced to 4,650 personnel (while officially remaining at the original figure), lowering total costs from US$700 million to US$446 million.

Another issue to emerge was uncertainty as to UNTAG's chain of command. This was to impact upon the already problematic communications between New York and the field headquarters, as well as adversely affecting communication between the several components of the mission in Namibia.[6] Unwieldy procurement procedures, which obliged UNTAG to forgo the purchasing of material from nearby South Africa so as to maintain adherence to international sanctions, and a lack of logistics in the field were further obstacles.[7] Despite this, the picture of the mission was one of co-operation and successful co-ordination between its different elements.

The first, and most dangerous, crisis came in the early days of the mission with the unexpected infiltration of hundreds of SWAPO guerrillas into Namibia from their bases over the border. SWAPO contended that the intention of the incursion was merely to move its forces into Namibia as part of the larger demobilization exercise, while South African officials declared it to be an outright violation of the terms of the peace agreement. Though UNTAG had already been alerted to the possibility of SWAPO incursions at least a month before it actually took place, it was clear that neither New York nor the field office in Windhoek had made provisions for this contingency.[8] Faced with the prospect of unilateral action on the part of South Africa, UNTAG agreed to allow the SADF to suspend its confinement and respond to the incursion by releasing six battalions. Over 200 SWAPO members were killed and, after a meeting of the Tripartite Commission, it was announced that SWAPO would return to its bases outside Lubango in Angola under UNTAG escort.[9] By 13 May, the cease-fire was back in place.

Another issue which clouded the demilitarization process was the incorporation of Koevoet into the police force which had, inexplicably, won

UN approval in advance of the UNTAG mission. Complaints by the civil
police contingent CIVPOL, whose task it was to pair up with SWAPOL, as
to both the conduct of Koevoet and that of the police in general provoked a
crisis.[10] After much negotiation, Ahtisaari, the SRSG and Pienaar, the
Administrator-General, worked out a compromise which saw Koevoet
members leave the police and CIVPOL numbers increase substantially to
1,500.[11]

Much of the formal disarmament and demobilization process was
effectively run outside the UNTAG framework with the UN playing the role
of observer or monitor. In the case of SWAPO, disarmament took place in
Angola and Zambia, followed by registration of repatriated refugees,
including former guerrillas, at selected assembly areas over a seven-day
period. As noted above, the SWATF disbanded in advance of the UNTAG
mission and, though its arms were stored on South African military bases,
the UN had difficulty gaining access to these facilities to verify their
contents.[12]

Despite continued reports of intimidation and covert South African
assistance to an anti-SWAPO coalition, the elections went ahead on
schedule. With nearly all eligible Namibians voting, SWAPO was elected to
power with 57 per cent support compared with the Democratic Tumhalle
Alliance's (DTA) 28.5 per cent, while the smaller parties picked up the rest
of the votes.[13] The UNTAG mission, the UN's first significant post-Cold
War peace-support operation, was viewed as a success by the international
community.

Angola and UNAVEM II

In the case of Angola, the UN peace-support operation was reconstituted
three times. UNAVEM I, running from 1989 to 1991, was complementary
to the UNTAG mission in Namibia and monitored the withdrawal of Cuban
troops from Angola. UNAVEM II, created in the wake of the successful
implementation of both UNAVEM I and UNTAG, was a more ambitious
mission that undertook both a monitoring and, in some instances,
facilitating role in what was to have been Angola's transition from war to
peace. UNAVEM II's failure, exacerbated by a host of mitigating
circumstances, cast a shadow over the UN's ability to conduct multi-
dimensional peace-support operations in southern Africa.

The Peace Agreement and Demilitarization

The signing of the New York Accords in December 1988, which included
provisions for the withdrawal of Cuban troops from Angola and South
African forces from Namibia, was to lead to the first direct UN involvement

in Angola. Responding to a request by the Angolan and the Cuban government on 20 December 1988, the SC passed SCR 626 (1988) establishing a UN mission to verify the withdrawal process in Angola. In this capacity, UNAVEM I oversaw the departure of 50,000 Cuban soldiers, a process which was scheduled to take 30 months. In order to complete its assignment, UNAVEM I was assigned a team totalling 70 military observers under the command of Brigadier General Pericles Ferreira Gomes, the Chief Military Observer. Operating from January 1989 to May 1991, the UN mission was able to complete the pull-out of Cuban troops ahead of the stipulated timetable of July 1991.

The failure of the Angolan government's 1991 offensive against the União Nacional para a Independência Total de Angola (UNITA) stronghold in the south-eastern corner of the country, underscored the inability of either party to secure victory through force of arms. At the sixth round of the peace talks sponsored by the Portuguese, the Angolan parties finally agreed to a comprehensive settlement which included a cease-fire, demobilization and the country's first democratic elections.

The Acordos de Paz para Angola, or Bicesse Accords, were signed on 1 May 1991 in Portugal. They consisted of:

- a cease-fire between the government and UNITA, set to take effect on 31 May 1991 and to be administered by a Joint Commission staffed by both parties and monitored by the UN;

- the demobilization of government and UNITA troops and their integration into a unified national military, to be completed in advance of the elections;

- elections to be scheduled between September and November 1992 and monitored by the international community;

- In a further agreement, known as the 'triple zero option', neither side was permitted to purchase new armaments and the international community was charged with ensuring that no transgressions occurred.

In order to implement the peace agreement, the Bicesse Accords established a series of commissions to administer the introduction of its provisions. A Joint Political-Military Commission (CCPM), staffed by senior representatives from the government and UNITA, was created to manage the implementation of the peace agreement. The representatives from Portugal, the United States and the Soviet Union were given observer status on the commission, while the UN was confined to the position of an 'invited guest'. Linked to it was the Joint Commission for the Verification and Control of the Cease-fire (CMVF), set up to oversee the cease-fire process and the Joint Commission on the Formation of the Angolan Armed Forces (CCFA).[14]

The success of the withdrawal process encouraged the two main Angolan adversaries, the government and UNITA, to request further UN assistance in the fulfilment of their own bilateral peace process. Although the UN had acted as an observer to the negotiations at Bicesse, its role in the structuring of the peace process had been severely circumscribed in the final agreement. UNITA had wanted a strong UN presence with substantial powers in the country, while the Angolan government, anxious to uphold its sovereignty, sought to limit the UN role.[15] The end result was that the position of the UN in the process would be limited to monitoring and verifying a range of demilitarization measures. These were:

• the end of hostilities between the government and UNITA by 15 May 1991;

• the cantonment of all military forces to designated assembly areas by 1 August 1991;

• the demobilization of all military forces, including the collection and disposal of weapons;

• the creation of a new national army; and

• the establishment of the neutrality of the national police force, especially with regard to its fulfilment of human rights provisions.

UNAVEM and Demilitarization

The demilitarization programme in Angola was essentially short-term in emphasis, although there were some provisions made for long-term objectives. The short-term programme focused on the demobilization and disarmament of combatants through a supervised process which included a limited UN monitoring role. This heavily circumscribed UN role was one of the factors which contributed both to the collapse of the demilitarization programme and the popular perception of UNAVEM failure. As for the long-term components of demilitarization, provisional plans were made for targeted programmes that undertook the training of ex-combatants, but these were neither integrated into a broad-based approach to reintegration nor were they able to operate with the outbreak of fighting.

UNAVEM's involvement in Angola's programme for demilitarisation centred on monitoring the cease-fire, ensuring the neutrality of the national police force, observing the process of demobilization and supporting the formation of a new national army. Marshalling its limited human and financial resources to this task, UNAVEM created teams of observers who were attached to 'counterpart' teams of government and UNITA representatives established by the several commissions in the six regions of the country. Their role was to check whether the Angolans were carrying out their tasks in a fair and unbiased fashion – there were no enforcement provisions as such provided for in the Bicesse Accords and certainly none available direct to UNAVEM.

The verification of the cease-fire was the responsibility of the CMVF. The CMVF sent teams to each of the 50 assembly areas and 32 'critical points'. Where possible, UNAVEM military observers were attached to the assembly areas, while the designated critical points, ports and other areas which could serve as conduits for weaponry were permanently staffed by UNAVEM observers. In addition, UNAVEM developed a mobile reaction team to investigate violations in either those areas in which it had no permanent presence or the places outside its established monitoring remit.

Monitoring the conduct of the national police was another responsibility of the CMVF. With only 89 monitors to call upon, it was immediately obvious that UNAVEM would not be in a position to fulfil its stated duties. In a belated and inadequate response, the strength of the UN police observer contingent was increased in May 1992 to 126.[16]

Demobilization was the responsibility of a working group formed by the CCPM. The programme for demobilization called for the cantonment of the Government's Forças Armandas Popular para a Libertação de Angola (FAPLA) and UNITA's Forças Armandas para a Libertação de Angola (FALA) forces at 50 designated assembly areas by 1 August 1992. Once in place, the majority of the estimated 120,000 FAPLA troops and 65,000 FALA troops would be disarmed and brought into civilian life. At the same time, an equal number of soldiers from both sides, numbering 50,000, would be assigned to the new army, the Forças Armada Angolanas (FAA). Training for those selected for service with the FAA would be the responsibility of Britain, France and Portugal, under the general supervision of the CCPM. UNAVEM officials, operating in teams of two, were to be posted at each of the assembly areas where the FAPLA and the FALA were to gather. Notably, while some financial support targeting the demobilized soldier's integration into civilian life had been mooted in parts of the international donor community, no concrete provisions for its disbursement had been developed at this late stage.

Implementation

The process established by UNAVEM for the investigation of alleged cease-fire violations proved to be inadequate. This was compounded by the slow deployment of UNAVEM observers, caused both by delays in New York and difficulties created by the two parties, which meant that the verification of demobilization and disarmament was not fully operational until 30 September 1991. Nevertheless, open hostilities were by and large suspended during the build-up to the elections in late September 1992.

The neutrality of the national police force was a source of major dissent between the government and UNITA. The creation of the Rapid Intervention Police, popularly known as the Ninjas, invoked severe criticism from UNITA officials, as it was outside the established demilitarization programme. Trained by the notorious Spanish Guarda Civil, the Rapid Intervention Police was composed of several military units drawn from the army and the security forces and numbered approximately 4,000.

The demobilization of Angolan soldiers was a dismal failure. Conditions in the assembly areas were appalling, lacking all the necessary prerequisites such as proper shelter, food and water. Rioting government soldiers, protesting at the absence of basic necessities in these areas and the slowness of the demobilization process, threatened a spontaneous demobilization. The unwillingness of the government to provide the necessary transportation and food for the assembled troops proved to be a major stumbling block in the demobilization process. Insufficient controls for monitoring the movement of troops, exacerbated by a shortage of personnel, caused UNAVEM to resort to weekly estimates of encamped troops, rendering UN monitoring irrelevant.

In contrast to FAPLA, UNITA forces remained largely disciplined and under central control. However, the leadership proved to be generally unwilling to engage its troops in the demobilization process. UNITA cited the lack of preparation on the part of the international community for the integration of its troops into civilian life as a reason for its holding back from the process.[17] The difficulties of gaining access to UNITA-controlled territory further impeded UNAVEM in its efforts to keep abreast of the situation in the field.

Despite these shortcomings, by May 1992 70 per cent of the 160,000 soldiers were in the assembly areas, but of these only 6,000 had actually been demobilized.[18] By June, the figure had increased to 20,000, with 85 per cent of UNITA troops in place and 37 per cent of government forces in the assembly areas. By 7 October (a week after the election) UNAVEM officials claimed that 96,620 FAPLA troops had been demobilized.[19]

Accusations and counter-accusations of violation of the demobilization process increased as the deadline for the disarming of Angolan troops neared. As noted above, UNITA claimed that the government converted several military units into paramilitary units and placed them under the control of the national police. At the same time, the government reported that UNITA was illegally holding 20,000 troops in reserve in Cuango Cubango province. A UNAVEM investigation team subsequently verified that several hundred FALA troops unaccounted for were, in fact, in that area but, due to the lack of UN personnel, it was not possible to bring them into the demobilization process.[20]

Linked to the problems of demobilization were obstacles hampering the establishment of the new national military. These included a lack of or inadequate facilities for soldiers, apparently a result of both the illegal sale of government property by the military and the reallocation of resources to the training and equipping of the Rapid Intervention Police.[21] Despite the failure to move forward in establishing a new national army, to maintain the facade of adherence to the Bicesse Accords the government and UNITA held an official ceremony on 27 September 1992 inaugurating the FAA.[22]

Against this increasingly sombre background, over 90 per cent of eligible Angolans voted in the election, with Jose Eduardo dos Santos, the former government leader, winning 49.6 per cent of the votes and Jonas Savimbi (UNITA) 40 per cent in the presidential race. The Movimento Popular de Libertação de Angola (MPLA) secured 54 per cent of the votes to UNITA's 34 per cent for seats in the legislature. Short of the requisite 50 per cent required for the presidency, the two leaders were obliged to conduct a run-off election; this was never to happen. Savimbi, claiming fraud, mobilized his troops and began a military campaign in early October to consolidate UNITA positions. Within a few weeks Luanda itself was gripped by fighting as the government launched a counter-strike against UNITA. Persistent efforts by UN officials to broker a cease-fire between the two warring factions came to naught and by the end of January 1993, the Secretary-General observed that a state of civil war existed. The continued violations of truces forced the reduction of UNAVEM II and the resignation of the SRSG in May 1993.

Mozambique and ONUMOZ

The demilitarization programme in Mozambique, in contrast to those in Namibia and Angola, adopted an approach which deliberately sought to link short-term objectives with long-term goals. Utilizing the international NGO community to a greater extent than in previous operations and cognizant of the recent debacle in Angola, ONUMOZ put together a co-ordinated effort which rivalled UNTAG in size but far exceeded it in scope.

The Peace Agreement and Demilitarization

The General Peace Agreement (GPA), signed by the government of Mozambique and the National Resistance Movement of Mozambique (RENAMO) in October 1992, called specifically for UN participation in monitoring the cease-fire, providing humanitarian assistance and monitoring the elections. The SRSG Aldo Ajello, in co-operation with the Western powers which had been party to the negotiations in Rome, convinced the government and RENAMO to establish formally the Supervising and Monitoring Commission (CSC) as the central authority overseeing the implementation of the GPA. The CSC's mandate included: the settling of disputes between the parties; questions of interpretation of the GPA; and a co-ordinating role for the subsidiary commissions to be established. The Cease-fire Commission (CCF), the Commission for the Reintegration of Demobilizing Military Personnel (CORE) and the Joint Commission for the Formation of the Mozambican Defence Force (CCFADM) were created to manage specific aspects of demilitarization.

The timetable set by the parties to the GPA was as follows:

- the cease-fire to commence 15 October 1993;

- demobilization to be completed by 1 April 1993, along with the subsequent formation of a new national army; and,

- elections to be held in October 1993.[23]

ONUMOZ and Demilitarization

The demilitarization programme employed by ONUMOZ sought to integrate the international community's efforts in supporting short- and long-term demilitarization. Short-term components included the monitoring of the cease-fire and the supervision of the demobilization of combatants. Long-term components focused on projects which targeted ex-combatants, including provisions for a two-year subsidy, job referral and training programmes.

Underlying the UN's demilitarization plan was the desire to separate the demobilization process from that of the electoral process.[24] And, in contrast to UNAVEM II, sufficient financial and human resources were made available to fulfil these objectives.

Monitoring the withdrawal of foreign troops from Mozambique, a condition RENAMO had insisted upon at Rome, was the first task of the UN demilitarization programme. It was decided to bring 7,500 UN peacekeeping troops into the country to monitor their departure and take up positions along the transport corridors. The CCF, composed of the Mozambican parties, representatives of the international community and ONUMOZ, worked to ensure that peace was maintained in the rest of the territory.

The demobilization of combatants formed the second part of ONUMOZ's involvement in demilitarization. A specialized unit attached to the mission planned and implemented demobilization. A team of four UN personnel was assigned to each of the 49 assembly areas, where they were to oversee the process, including the registration of combatants, disarmament, the selection of soldiers for the new army and formal demobilization. Education, entertainment and general logistical arrangements were also their responsibility.

The final short-term component of demilitarization was the creation of a new national army. It was initially envisaged that this would consist of 30,000 soldiers, equally divided between former government and former RENAMO troops and would be trained by the British, French and Portuguese.[25]

The long-term component of demilitarization – the Information Referral Service (IRS) and the Reintegration Support Scheme (RSS) – fell under the auspices of the UN Office for Humanitarian Assistance Co-ordination (UNOHAC). The IRS was conceived as a mechanism for providing demobilized soldiers with access to information on the job market, as well as basic information on aspects of the reintegration programme. Originally falling under the auspices of CORE – which proved to be ineffective – its 11 provincial offices were actually run by the International Organization for Migration (IOM).[26] Using a trust fund administered by the UNDP, the RSS was to provide demobilized soldiers with 18 months of subsidies in the form of cash disbursements given at local branches of the Banco Popular de Desenvolvimento.[27] By providing a reasonable assurance of financial support for an extended period, it was hoped that the former combatants would find employment in their districts and, concurrently, integrate into the local community. To assist in this process vocational kits consisting of agricultural tools, seeds and food rations for up to three months were given to demobilized soldiers upon departure from the assembly areas. UNOHAC used a host of development and refugee support agencies to implement these programmes.

Finally, the monitoring of the conduct of the election campaign was the responsibility of CIVPOL. Numbering 128 personnel and later expanded to 1,114, CIVPOL was attached to Mozambican police units to ensure that the electoral process was conducted in an atmosphere free from intimidation and, concurrently, that the human rights of citizens were respected.

Implementation

With a six-month delay in bringing the mission up to full strength in Mozambique, a new timetable had to be set which called for: the concentration of troops in the assembly areas to begin in September 1993, with full demobilization to be completed in May 1994; the new army to be operational by September 1994; and the election to take place in October 1994.

The first step in implementing[28] the demilitarization programme was to bring in UN peacekeeping forces to monitor the withdrawal of Zimbabwe and Malawi troops. Despite delays that held up their introduction until August 1993, a total of 6,000 peacekeepers were finally put into place. Concurrently with the introduction of UN troops was the monitoring of the cease-fire between the government and RENAMO by the CCF. As the majority of violations involved unauthorized troop movements rather than shooting incidents, the task of monitoring was confined to assessing territorial and positional claims.[29]

The next phase of demilitarization, the demobilization of government and RENAMO troops, proved to be exceedingly problematic. In an especially ambiguous passage, the GPA had allowed for 'dual administration' of territory controlled by the government and RENAMO, thus leading to conflicts over everything from internal movement and taxation to the siting of the assembly areas. As a result it was not until November 1993 that 20 of the 49 areas were officially opened to receive troops, while the rest did not become operational until February 1994.[30] The slow pace of demobilization, a product of lengthy indecision and confrontation by the Mozambican parties, fuelled dissent among combatants housed within the assembly areas. Months of confinement in the monotony of the camps gave way to demonstrations and riots, which targeted both local military and UN officials.[31]

With pressure to commence demobilization from both the international donor community and the soldiers themselves, ONUMOZ decided that the first demobilizations should take place in mid March 1994. The assembly phase was completed on 15 August, in spite of uneven co-operation from the government and RENAMO, with the final total of registered soldiers being over 86,000.[32] Nevertheless, approximately 5,000 government and 2,000 RENAMO troops remained outside the official demobilization process.[33]

The establishment of the Forças Armadas de Defensa de Mocambique (FADM) was another contentious aspect of the demilitarization programme. The instruction of trainers was slow to start, while joint command of the new army was only agreed upon in January 1994 and 80 officers were appointed in June to command the newly created infantry battalions. Delays in the supply of new equipment and the renovation of inadequate training facilities, coupled with the prolonged process of identifying new soldiers, forced the compression of training into six weeks. Unhappiness over the prospect of being forced to continue in the military brought about strikes and desertions.[34] By election time in October 1994, fewer than 10,000 soldiers had completed their training and Mozambican officials were lowering the target size for the FADM to 15,000 at arms.

The long-term component of demilitarization, introducing measures for the long-term maintenance of the demobilized troops, was taken up by UNOHAC's IRS and its RSS. With the able assistance of IOM, which played the principal role in reintegration as CORE failed to materialize, the transportation of demobilized soldiers and their dependents to their chosen destinations occurred with minimal problems. The subsidy scheme commenced without significant hitches, while the IRS offices received numerous enquiries and assisted in job placement.

The elections of October 1994 were marred by one last crisis. The RENAMO leader Afonso Dhlakama pulled his party out hours before the polling was to begin; however, concerted pressure on the part of the Western powers and the Southern African Development Community (SADC) leadership caused him to reverse his decision. The result was a turnout of over 85 per cent and the election of the government's candidate Joaquim Chissano to the presidency by a margin of 53 per cent. In the legislative elections, FRELIMO won 129 seats to RENAMO's 112, with the rest of the seats going to smaller parties. Declaring the mission a resounding success, ONUMOZ withdrew from Mozambique by late December.

Conclusion: The Future of Demilitarization and UN Peacebuilding

If the southern African cases examined here are to serve as any guide, it is principally to suggest that the issue of the military and the UN's role in the demilitarization process, deserves renewed consideration on a number of levels.

First, demilitarization knows no boundaries. To cite but a few examples, some of the demobilized soldiers from Koevoet were to reappear as UNITA soldiers after the collapse of the Angolan peace agreement. In Mozambique, official disarmament proved to be hopelessly inadequate, with a further 22,000 arms unearthed from 146 undeclared weapons caches and many arms finding their way into neighbouring South Africa and Zimbabwe.[35]

The successful transformation of the regional heritage of conflict, especially at a military level, requires an atmosphere of active and institutionalized co-operation between the states of southern Africa. An approach which is predicated upon an understanding of economic asymmetry and porous borders in the region would, in all likelihood, stand a better chance of minimizing post-conflict problems than one which treats each conflict as a discrete, state-based phenomenon. To cite two examples: programmes which seek to co-ordinate the disarmament phase of demilitarization with an increase in cross-border surveillance would, it is to be hoped, act to stem the traffic in small arms; equally, it is reasonable to assume that economies of scale could be achieved in developing a regional approach to the costly task of de-mining. The preliminary structures emerging out of the SADC framework are a significant step towards providing a forum for devising regional strategies to address post-conflict management issues.[36] In this regard it is possible in future settings for the international community, and in particular the UN system, through the initiation of a short- and a long-term demilitarization programme integrated across state boundaries, to make a stronger commitment to the promotion of a favourable environment for tackling the post-conflict problems of demilitarization on a regional basis.

Secondly, implementation of demilitarization programmes requires not only conceptual clarity as to the emergency/development continuum but on-going co-ordination between the UN and the international donor and NGO community. Emergency and development issues are generally well understood in terms of the actual conceptualization of demilitarization programmes; this may be readily seen in the sophisticated approach to demilitarization applied during the ONUMOZ mission. However, to translate that into a co-ordinated approach that effectively pools the resources of the relevant UN and non-UN agencies, as well as the host government and donors, is still proving to be problematic. In fact, while the three case studies cited here seem to present a picture of deepening co-operation and co-ordination both within the UN system and the NGO community, events in Angola indicate a disturbing trend away from that approach. UCAH, the local co-ordinating body established by the Department of Humanitarian Affairs (DHA) in Luanda, maintains its distance from UNAVEM III, while the NGOs are at pains to ensure their independence of action from UCAH.[37] Enduring institutional biases keep the international community from acting effectively in collaborating in demilitarization. Furthermore, the tendency of the UN and the NGOs to introduce elements into demilitarization programmes which can only be construed as self-serving (for instance, promoting the inclusion of a component into a demilitarization programme whose sole virtue is that it matches the institution's selected expertise) endangers what is frequently a volatile situation.

And thirdly, further analysis of the long-term component of demilitarization needs to be undertaken. Studies by the World Bank and private consultancy firms do not as yet provide sufficient evidence to state unequivocally that the utilization of a targeted approach to reintegration is the most efficacious policy.[38] These preliminary findings, especially as they rely heavily on case studies where reintegration programmes are in progress, should be treated with caution. The selection of target groups whose status carries on into the post-conflict period can act to reaffirm the ex-combatant's identity and give him a sense of entitlement and expectations that is beyond the means of the post-conflict state to fulfil. A particularly vivid example of this is the Namibian government's belated formulation of Development Brigades, with its severe cost implications and attendant social problems, and is a marked failure of the targeting of ex-combatants.[39] At the same time, it is readily understood that for many soldiers, resort to arms – whether in the form of military service or banditry – is the only real means of 'employment' available to them. A programme which actively responds to the immediate financial and employment needs of former combatants while recognizing the longer-term imperative of social integration would be ideal. An early version of Mozambique's RSS, which provided incremental financial assistance over a set period and effectively linked such support to a fixed domicile, was a noteworthy effort to couple targeting concerns with the promotion of integration into the local community.[40] With the future of multi-dimensional peace-support operations of the kind cited here in question, perhaps it is important to reaffirm a central issue regarding the UN and demilitarization. Succinctly put, should UN peace-support operations be involved in the long-term component of demilitarization? The answer is a qualified yes. The overlap between the short- and the long-term components of demilitarization, whether it is in the area of the linkage of the demobilization process to reintegration measures or of developing local capacity to manage long-term reintegration projects, necessitates integrated planning in demilitarization. And it is logical to assume that a co-ordinating authority, such as the UN, would serve as an integral part of that process. However, with its uneven record in southern Africa and elsewhere, the logic of the centrality of UN involvement is less appealing. For demilitarization to succeed against all the odds – and the post-conflict state is rife with crippling problems – it needs a better UN than the one we have today.

ACKNOWLEDGEMENT

The author would like to thank the MacAuthor Foundation for its generous support of this research.

NOTES

1. See World Bank, *Demobilization and Reintegration of Military Personnel in Africa: the Evidence From Seven Country Case Studies*, Africa Regional Studies Report No.IDP–130, Washington, DC, 1993; and Chris Alden, 'Swords into Plowshares? The United Nations and Demilitarization in Mozambique', *International Peacekeeping*, Summer 1995, No.2, pp.175–6.
2. Boutros Boutros-Ghali, *An Agenda for Peace*, New York: United Nations, 1995, p.61.
3. Undoubtedly the clearest expression of this overlap between the immediate concerns of peacekeeping and those of development may be found in the area of de-mining. Landmines pose an immediate obstacle to the implementation of peace treaty provisions, while at the

same time inhibiting long-term developmental goals such as agricultural regeneration.

4. Interview with Aldo Ajello, 16 Sept. 1994.
5. It should be noted that disarmament and confinement to bases was organized through UNAVEM I, while repatriation was linked to the UNHCR's programme.
6. See *UNTAG: Description and Analysis of the Mission's Operational Arrangement*, draft, 9 Sept. 1991, pp.265–6.
7. Ibid., pp.263–8.
8. Private communication.
9. The Tripartite Commission was established by the Brazzaville Protocol of 1988 and included South Africa, Angola and Cuba, with the United States and the Soviet Union serving as observers.
10. See *UNTAG* (n.6), pp.208–9.
11. V. Fortna, 'United Nations Transition Assistance Group in Namibia', in W. Durch (ed.), *The Evolution of UN Peacekeeping: Case Studies and Comparative Analysis*, New York: St. Martins Press, 1993, p.359.
12. Interview with Omar Halim, Deputy Chief of Staff, UNTAG, 16 Mar. 1996.
13. Association of Western European Parliamentarians for Africa (hereafter AWEPA), *Consolidation of Democracy in Namibia*, AWEPA Electoral Observer Mission, Dec. 1994, Amsterdam: African-European Institute, 1995, pp.7–9.
14. A. Vines, 'Angola and Mozambique: the Aftermath of Conflict', *Conflict Studies*, No.280, London: Research Institute for the Study of Conflict and Terrorism, May/June 1995, p.12.
15. M. Anstee, 'Angola: the Forgotten Tragedy – a Test Case for UN Peacekeeping', *International Relations*, Vol.XI, No.6, Dec. 1993, p.497.
16. 'United Nations Angola Verification Mission II', *United Nations Peacekeeping Operations: Information Notes, 1993 Update*, No.2, New York: United Nations, Nov. 1993, p.26.
17. Vines (n.14), p.9.
18. Ibid., p.110.
19. 'United Nations Angola Verification Mission II' (n.16), p.21.
20. World Bank (n.1), p.41.
21. Vines (n.14), p.10.
22. Human Rights Watch/Africa, *Angola: Arms Trade and Violations of the Laws of War since the 1992 Elections*, New York: Human Rights Watch, 1994, p.13.
23. AWEPA, *General Peace Agreement 1992*. Amsterdam: AWEPA/African-European Institute, 1992, pp.34–6, 42–4, 48–50, 56–64.
24. Interview with Ton Pardoel, Chief Technical Unit Officer, ONUMOZ, Maputo, Mozambique, 26 May 1994.
25. AWEPA (n.23), p.30.
26. IOM press release, Maputo, 24 May 1994.
27. Each government and RENAMO soldier received six months of his regular salary, plus bonuses (a minimum of 75,000 meticais) from the government, with half of that given to him at the point of official demobilization and half in the district of resettlement.
28. For a full account of implementation, see C. Alden (n.1).
29. AWEPA, *Mozambique Peace Process Bulletin*, Aug. 1993, No.5, p.5.
30. An additional difficulty was the issue of the government's paramilitary forces – something not adequately addressed in the GPA. Estimated to number 155,000, government militias were scattered across the rural areas, often only nominally under the authority of district or provincial officials. It was only in Jan. 1994 that they actually begun to disarm with two-thirds of their number demobilized by July. Interview with Colonel Pier Segala, Cease-Fire Commission, Maputo, 14 Sept. 1994.
31. See CCF, 'Problems/Incidents in Assembly Areas and Other Areas', ONUMOZ, Maputo, Sept. 1994.
32. *Africa Confidential*, Vol.35, No.19, 23 Sept. 1994, pp.3–4.
33. Ibid., p.4 and interviews with senior ONUMOZ officials.
34. AWEPA, *Mozambique Peace Process Bulletin*, July 1994, No.10, p.5.
35. *Africa Recovery*, Dec. 1994, p.14.
36. The Inter-State Defence and Security Committee, which grew out of a Front Line States

(FLS) initiative, is one example; the controversial Association of Southern African States (ASAS) is another. J. Cilliers, 'Towards Collaborative and Co-operative Security in Southern Africa: the OAU and SADC', in J. Cilliers and M. Reichart (eds.), *About Turn: the Transformation of the South African Military and Intelligence*, Pretoria: Institute for Defence Policy, 1996, pp.208–16.

37. Interviews with senior UCAH and NGO officials in Luanda, 12–14 Aug. 1995.
38. See, for example: World Bank (n.1); R. Muscat, 'Conflict and Reconstruction: Roles for the World Bank', policy paper, Washington, DC, 21 Nov. 1995; Creative Associates, 'Other Countries Experiences in Demobilisation and Reintegration of Ex-Combatants', workshop proceedings and case-study findings, Washington, DC, Mar. 1995.
39. See O. Angula, 'Development Brigades: New Deal to Train the Forgotten', *Namibia: Development Briefing*, Vol.2, Nos.10/11, Apr./May 1993, p.3; S. Shikangalah, 'Development Brigades: the Namibian Experience', in J. Cilliers (ed.), *Dismissed: Demobilisation, and Reintegration of Former Combatants in Africa*, Pretoria: Institute for Defence Policy, 1996, pp.70–1.
40. This clause was altered in the final version, allowing ex-combatants to change the bank which administered their subsidy to accommodate those individuals who wished to move residence.

A Peacekeeper's Perspective of Peacebuilding in Somalia

OMAR HALIM

After eradicating the humanitarian sufferings of the Somali people in early 1993, the international community launched a peacekeeping mission with a variety of peacebuilding components. However, due to the conflict with certain Somali factions at the outset, the United Nations Mission in Somalia II (UNOSOM II) was not able to fulfil its peacebuilding objectives. This article argues that reconciliation and peace are prerequisites for these efforts and that disarmament is an indispensable first step to longer-term peace. Conversely, it further argues that peacebuilding is a *sine qua non* for a mission which aims to establish a long-lasting peace in a war-devastated country. Finally, if the international community is serious in assisting a country, it must be prepared to commit itself fully financially since peacekeeping and peacebuilding are expensive.

This article examines UN peacebuilding in Somalia. As a starting point, it is as well to establish what is meant by peacebuilding. The UN Secretary-General Boutros Boutros-Ghali provides an authoritative definition in *An Agenda for Peace* when he describes it as:

> action to identify and support structures which will tend to strengthen and solidify peace in order to avoid a relapse into conflict...rebuilding the institutions and infrastructures of nations torn by civil war and strife [and addressing the] deepest causes of conflict: economic despair, social injustice and political oppression.[1]

The international community expanded its assistance to include reconciliation and peacebuilding programmes in Somalia following the success of the United States-led Unified Task Force (UNITAF) in facilitating the delivery of humanitarian supplies to the affected Somalis early in 1993. However, the programmes encountered problems when they were formulated and implemented without the benefit of close consultations with Somali leaders. This led to misunderstandings and non-co-operation by some of them. In addition, the mission which started with so much promise was not able to deal with all Somali parties impartially. Soon after it took over from UNITAF in May 1993, the United Nations Mission in Somalia II

Omar Halim is a Research Associate in the Centre for Strategic and International Studies, Jakarta.

went to war with some Somali factions, mistakenly perceiving this as a peace-enforcement action.

Facing the opposition of certain Somali factions, UNOSOM II was not able to implement fully its peacebuilding programmes. This was obvious in its attempt to assist in the re-establishment of Somali political and administrative institutions, the police and the judicial system. The sections of the article that follow will discuss the context within which the UNOSOM II mandate was decided upon; the achievements and problems it faced in implementing its programmes; and some lessons that may be learned regarding future peacekeeping missions. In terms of Somalia this included the need to have comprehensive understandings with local leaders, including faction leaders, regarding the mission's mandate and its implementation (including the disarmament programme) and the requirement to have fully-funded, peacebuilding programmes, if the country were not to relapse into conflict after the mission had completed its work.

The Somalia Mandate

In mid 1992 Somalia was facing the dislocations resulting from civil war – population displacement, destruction of infrastructure and the control of food by armed combatants – and a severe drought that led to famine of frightening proportions. The establishment of UNOSOM I, followed by the deployment of UNITAF in late 1992, were responses of the international community to aid the provision of assistance to the Somali people through UN agencies and international non-governmental organizations (NGOs).

As UNITAF was rapidly succeeding in overcoming starvation, the UN resumed its mediation efforts to bring about a political settlement to the civil war, because:

> without national reconciliation, involving the establishment of viable political structures and the disarmament and demobilization of the factional militias and armed irregulars, all the progress towards ending hunger would inevitably remain precarious and economic recovery would remain largely impossible.[2]

It should be noted that the mission was decided upon when the thinking or mood internationally was imbued with:

> a palpable optimism that the [Security] Council and the world body in general would at last be able to fulfil the promise of the Charter – 'to save succeeding generations from the scourge of war'.[3]

UNOSOM II was therefore established with a broad mandate, which included: political reconciliation; the building of political and administrative structures; disarmament and demobilization of fighters; enforcement of the arms embargo from within Somalia; the re-establishment of the Somali police force and justice system; the return of refugees and internally-displaced persons; de-mining; and rehabilitation and reconstruction.[4] In short, the mission was tasked to assist the Somalis in their reconciliation and peacebuilding efforts. Indeed, the Permanent Representative of the United States was quoted as describing UNOSOM II as:

> an unprecedented enterprise aimed at nothing less than the restoration of an entire country as a proud, functioning and viable member of the community of nations.[5]

The Security Council (SC) adopted resolution 814 (1993), establishing UNOSOM II, on 26 March 1993. However, it made no specific references to the issues being negotiated and agreed upon by the Somali leaders concurrently meeting in Addis Ababa. The Somali agreement was signed one day after the adoption of the SC resolution. The UN tasks envisaged by the SC and by the Somali political leaders did overlap in general terms but, since there were no close consultations between them, differences in the interpretation of how these tasks were to be fulfilled arose during the implementation period, and this led to the difficulties faced by UNOSOM II later on.

However, it should have been noted at the outset that from the time of its political independence from the British and Italian colonial powers in 1960, and through the periods of the parliamentary system in the 1960s and military government in the 1970s and the 1980s, Somalia has not been able to develop a national socio-political system capable of overcoming the deep divisions caused by the traditional clan form of social organization. The increasing dominance of the Marehan/Darod clan in the military during the Mohamed Siad Barre period; the suppression of the Isaak clan in the north-west which resulted in the proclamation of the 'Republic of Somaliland' in May 1991; and the civil war of the 1990s have all exacerbated this division further. Any strategy to assist the Somalis to redevelop their political and administrative institutions must therefore bear this in mind.

Re-establishment of Somali Political Institutions

Besides the task of promoting and advancing political reconciliation, UNOSOM II was assigned by the SC the responsibility to assist in the re-establishment of national and regional institutions and civil administration in the entire country.[6] In this regard, the Addis Ababa Agreement of 27 March 1993 (henceforth, Addis Ababa Agreement) stipulated that the political and administrative structures to be built during the transitional period of two years were: a Transitional National Council; Central

Administrative Departments; and Regional and District Councils. However, there were differences in the UNOSOM II and the Somali interpretations of how to form some of these institutions.

The UNOSOM II approach of forming district and regional councils conformed to the Addis Ababa Agreement, which stipulated that:

> District council members shall be appointed through election or through consensus-based selection in accordance with Somali traditions [and] the district councils in each region shall send representatives who will constitute the regional councils.

By the end of 1993, UNOSOM II had certified 53 district councils (out of 81 districts, excluding the north-west) and eight (out of 13 regions, excluding the north-west) regional councils.[7] But by then it had also become clear that the conflict between UNOSOM II and the Somali National Alliance (SNA) had made it practically impossible to complete the process of establishing all the district councils. Intensive attempts to form councils in the Wadajir and the Dharkenley district in south Mogadishu, for example, were not successful.

The methodology and procedures adopted in the selection of council members were primarily based on, 'consensus-based selection in accordance with Somali traditions', as stipulated in the Addis Ababa Agreement. However, UNOSOM II intervened when the criteria of selection of councillors – broad participation by all sectors of Somali society – were not met; there were no women selected in the original lists, for example. In addition, UNOSOM II had to mediate when there was a serious deadlock in the selection process, as in the Dinsor district.

Furthermore, the Transitional National Council, which was to be the highest political authority during the transitional period, was never established.[8] According to the Addis Ababa Agreement, this Council was to be composed of:

- three representatives from each of the 18 regions, including one woman from each;

- five additional seats for Mogadishu; and

- one nominee from each of the 15 political factions which signed the Agreement.

However, in the subsequent agreement they signed on 30 March 1993 (henceforth, Addis Ababa Agreement, 30 March), the same 15 political leaders stipulated that:

> given the 18 regions three representatives will be chosen by each

region and *names will be submitted to UNOSOM by the factions*
[emphasis added].

In the same Agreement, they stipulated further that in regions where there
was more than one faction, or differences between the factions in the
allocation of the seats, the concerned factions would try to settle their
differences in Addis Ababa. If not, they would iron them out in the regions.
Furthermore, in a later declaration, when the conflict between UNOSOM II
and SNA was over, leaders of the same factions concluded an agreement on
24 March 1994 in Nairobi to:

complete and review the formation of local authorities, where needed,
and establish them, where necessary, as a basis of regional autonomy
and respect for community rights.

This meant that the Somali political factions were intending to play a much
more crucial role than that envisaged by UNOSOM II in the formation of
the Transitional National Council, regional councils and district councils.[9]

In addition to the political problem, there was a resource constraint
which made it difficult for UNOSOM II to provide comprehensive support
to those councils already established. Since members of the district councils
did not necessarily belong to the groups of elders which traditionally
governed the local communities, they needed to be exposed to training
programmes on leadership, management and development. There was no
provision for these in the UNOSOM II budget. Fortunately, the Life and
Peace Institute of Sweden and the Eastern and Southern Africa
Management Institute were able to assist in organizing training workshops
for district councillors from eight regions. Administrative starter kits were
provided to district councils from assistance given by Nordic countries.[10]
Despite all this support, district and regional councils lacked the resources,
such as office facilities, salaries and vehicles to become operational.[11] This
lack of support for the functioning of these institutions created a great deal
of disappointment and frustration among the local communities.

Re-establishment of the Somali Justice System

The Secretary-General proposed the re-establishment of a Somali justice
system – police, judicial and penal systems – as a crucial step in creating a
secure environment in the country.[12] He even linked it to the concept of the
operations of the UNOSOM II military force, when he proposed that Phase
III – the phase in which the military activities and presence of UNOSOM II
could be scaled down – would end 'when a Somali national police force was
operational'.[13]

The SC approved the recommendations of the Secretary-General relating to the re-establishment of the institutions of justice, and requested the Secretary-General to:

> take the necessary steps on an urgent and accelerated basis to implement them [and urged] Member States, on an urgent basis, to contribute to the fund or otherwise to provide assistance.[14]

In other words, the resources required for this programme had to be obtained from voluntary contributions. Full financing was therefore not assured.

Police

The original UNOSOM II plan specified that a neutral police force was to be established comprising three tiers – national, regional and district – with police forces being answerable to appropriate local authorities in each tier.[15] UNOSOM II assistance was to cover salaries, limited renovation of police stations to render them operational, uniforms, vehicles, communications equipment and basic and specialized training.

These objectives seemed consistent with the Addis Ababa Agreement in which the Somali political leaders agreed on the need to establish an impartial National and Regional Somali Police Force in all regions of the country on an urgent basis through the reinstatement of the former Somali Police Force and the recruitment and training of young Somalis from all regions. The Agreement requested the assistance of the international community to do this.

However, in the end lack of financial resources made it necessary to reduce the contemplated force strength to 8,500, including 2,000 in the north-west. Only slightly more than 2,000 policemen had attended refresher courses, although UNOSOM II military assisted in providing courses in drill, weapons training, vehicle driving and maintenance, hygiene and sanitation.[16]

In addition, given the fact that Somalis have a clan-based society and the divisions were more accentuated at the time, it is not clear whether it would have been possible to establish a 'neutral' police force, as UNOSOM II intended, without consultations with the local parties. What subsequently happened was that in areas which were controlled by one clan or faction, such as the north-east, the equipping and training of policemen by UNOSOM II served to strengthen security.[17] However, in areas where there were more than one clan or faction, such as Benadir and Lower Juba, the provision of vehicles, communications equipment and weapons might have contributed to the accentuation of conflicts among clans/factions where reconciliation had not been fully achieved. This means that, in general terms, establishing a 'neutral' police force in a district is more feasible than at the regional or the national level.

Judicial and Penal System

Without full consultations with the Somali political leaders, UNOSOM II determined that, for the transitional period, and by 31 October 1993, an interim three-tier judicial system would be in place. The 1962 Somali Criminal Procedure and Penal Codes would also be enforced, while the Indian Penal Code and Criminal Procedure Code would be in force in the north-west.

It was determined that, upon request, UNOSOM military forces would provide security for judicial proceedings until local police forces were able to provide the required security. Finally, UNOSOM II went as far as stating that UNOSOM police and judicial advisers would assist the Somali justice system in investigating allegations of serious criminal violations, including 'crimes against the Somali people', and would help to facilitate the prosecution of criminals.[18]

In May 1993 one of General Aidid's top aides enquired why Somali judges in south Mogadishu (who were SNA-appointed) were being barred from the court houses and being replaced by UNOSOM judges. The absence of real consultations at the outset between UNOSOM II and the SNA with regard to the establishment of a Somali judicial system in Mogadishu has been considered to have contributed to their clash in June 1993.[19] After the departure of UNOSOM II in March 1995, it has been reported that many regions have adopted the Sharia law as the basis of their judicial system. UNOSOM II might have been imposing a judicial system which Somalis were not in favour of. In the proposed UNOSOM II budget, salaries and training were to be provided to judges, magistrates, prison staff and food to prisoners. Renovation of court facilities and prisons was also part of the UNOSOM II justice programme. By the end of the mission, UNOSOM II had assisted in the establishment of 11 appeals court, 11 regional courts and 46 district courts in 46 districts. The mission also supported 12 prisons, including the provision of food, water and medical services for inmates, and 672 custodial guards were certified and paid by UNOSOM II.[20]

The lack of financial resources and the slowness in the arrival of police and judicial advisers from contributing countries seriously hampered the implementation of the UNOSOM II justice programme. Furthermore, closer collaboration with district and regional councils in the establishment of police forces and a judicial system might have produced better results.

Disarmament and Demobilization

In the 15 January 1993 Addis Ababa Agreement (see below), it was agreed by the Somalis that:

> all heavy weaponry under the control of political movements shall be handed over to a cease-fire monitoring group for safekeeping until such time as a legitimate Somali Government can take them over.

This process was to be completed in March 1993 and the cease-fire monitoring group would be composed of UNITAF/UN troops. Furthermore, the Agreement stated that the militias of all political movements should be encamped in appropriate areas outside major towns where the encampments would not pose difficulties and that the encamped militias should be disarmed as soon as possible.[21]

In the Addis Ababa Agreement, the Somali leaders reiterated their commitment to the strict, effective and expeditious implementation of the Cease-fire/Disarmament Agreement signed on 8 and 15 January 1993, and affirmed that disarmament would be comprehensive, impartial and transparent. They further committed themselves to complete and simultaneous disarmament throughout the entire country and requested UNITAF/ UNOSOM to assist so as to achieve a substantial completion of the process within 90 days.

UNITAF/UNOSOM II, in turn, developed the following concept of disarmament:

- it would be 'continuous and irreversible'; in other words, once a faction had surrendered a weapon, it would not be entitled to reclaim it;

- throughout the process it would be useful to keep the major factional leaders informed about progress in disarming all the factions;

- to be effective the disarmament process should be enforceable; and

- cantonment sites were to be established, where heavy weapons would be stored, and transition sites, where militias would be given temporary accommodation while: turning in their small arms; registering for future governmental and non-governmental support; and receiving guidance and training for their eventual reintegration into civilian life.[22]

However, the concepts, timing, financing and responsibilities of both the Somali factions and UNOSOM II had not been fully agreed upon. Only limited disarmament had taken place by the time UNOSOM II took over responsibility for the mission on 4 May 1993. This was essentially due to the great reluctance of UNITAF – despite the urgings of the Secretary-General – to expand its mandate beyond providing a secure environment for humanitarian relief operations. Another reason was the fact that UNITAF troops were not deployed throughout the country. UNOSOM II, in inheriting such a difficult situation from UNITAF, and despite the lack of an intention to deploy troops throughout Somalia, prepared a four-phase disarmament plan:

- reconnaissance and designation of cease-fire zones, transition sites and heavy weapons cantonment sites;

- preparation of the disarmament sites;

- cantonment of heavy weapons; and

- disarmament and demobilization of militia forces in transition sites; to be followed by reintegration.

However, before these could be operationally developed, the 5 June 1993 clash between the SNA and the UN diverted UNOSOM II from a systematic, comprehensive and voluntary disarmament programme into the coercive disarmament of one political faction, which rendered the original disarmament plan unworkable. In addition, the fact that UNOSOM II troops were not generally deployed made it more difficult, or even impossible, to arrange for the voluntary disarmament of the militia forces in the north-east. Despite the Jubaland Peace Agreement which UNOSOM II brokered, disarmament did not take place in the south either. A certain amount of disarmament, demobilization and reintegration did occur in the north-west, organized by the regional administration of Mohamed Ibrahim Egal, but not under the supervision of UNOSOM II. UN agencies assisted this effort by providing technical assistance, food and some facilities in the Mandera camp.

Repatriation, Resettlement and De-mining

Because of the civil war and famine, it was estimated that as many as 1.7 million Somalis were forced to leave their homes. Of these over one million sought refuge in Ethiopia and Kenya. In 1993 it was reported that over 250,000 internally-displaced persons moved to Mogadishu, 60,000 to Kismayo and Baidoa, and the northern regions were supporting at least 250,000 internally-displaced persons and refugees.[23]

The relatively early return of peace to the north-west had generated spontaneous repatriation into the region from Ethiopia and Djibouti. The Office of the UN High Commissioner for Refugees (UNHCR) re-opened its office in Hargeisa to prepare for the planned repatriation of 300,000 refugees from eastern Ethiopia. By October 1992 100,000 were reported to have returned to Hargeisa, Burao and Berbera.[24] Lower and Middle Juba and Gedo regions were other areas to which a large number of refugees were returning from Kenya. By September 1995 it was reported that 300,000 Somali refugees were still registered in camps in Ethiopia, Djibouti and Eritrea, and another 157,000 were still registered in camps in Kenya. However, the outbreak of fighting in the north-west after November 1994 had caused a renewed exodus from that part of the country.[25]

In all, it was estimated that there were between 300,000 and 400,000 internally-displaced persons country-wide in 1994, with about 240,000 located in Mogadishu. In the end, UNOSOM II was perhaps able to assist in the resettlement of between 45,000 and 50,000.[26] It should be noted that, unlike the case of refugees, no specialized agency of the UN is responsible for the internally displaced. In Somalia they were the responsibility of the Humanitarian Division of UNOSOM II, assisted by the Civilian-Military Operations Centre (CMOC) of the military component.

In the north-west de-mining activities, which were funded by the United States, the European Community, the UNHCR and implemented by the Dutch branch of Medicins sans Frontieres lasted throughout 1993. Starting in 1994, UNOSOM II extended its programme into the north-west. It also modified its de-mining policy by providing contracts to Somali NGOs to de-mine.[27] These NGOs comprised members of several clans/factions who, after the end of the conflict between UNOSOM II and SNA at the end of 1993 and especially after the signing of the Nairobi Declaration in March 1994, were attempting to reach reconciliation with each other.[28] In the Mudug region in the north-east, for example, three projects were implemented by a Somali NGO which received full co-operation from the three factions controlling the area – SSDF, SNDU and SNA. However, UNOSOM II was never able to reach an agreement with the regional administration of the north-west – where most of the mines were supposed to be located – since the arrangement the Egal administration was proposing would have amounted to providing it with funds, without the necessary controls required by UN rules and procedures.

Rehabilitation and Reconstruction of Production Capacities

The scale of the humanitarian needs within Somalia, which prompted the intervention of the international community, are well known. By early 1992 almost 4.5 million people were threatened by severe malnutrition and malnutrition-related diseases. Of these, at least 1.5 million were immediately at risk, and it was estimated that 300,000 had already died since November 1991.[29]

The 100-Day Action Programme for Accelerated Humanitarian Assistance for Somalia was formulated to accelerate vitally required relief efforts and pave the way for the eventual recovery of Somali society. This

Programme, whose security was underwritten by UNITAF, had eight main components: the massive infusion of food aid; the rapid expansion of supplementary feeding; the provision of basic health services and a mass measles immunization campaign; the urgent provision of clean water, sanitation and hygiene; the provision of blankets and clothes; the simultaneous delivery of seeds, tools and animal vaccines along with food rations; the prevention of further refugee outflows and the promotion of the returnee programme; and institution-building and the rehabilitation of civil society and recovery. This was subsequently followed by the UN Relief and Rehabilitation Programme for Somalia between 1 March and 31 December 1993.

By mid 1993 starvation had largely been eradicated, although pockets of severe malnutrition could be found in certain isolated areas. Food aid was being increasingly targeted at the most vulnerable population groups and through 'food-for-work', linked to the rehabilitation of schools, hospitals, water, sanitation and other services; while wells were drilled and hand-pumps installed. By September 1993 51 schools had reopened in southern Somalia, and by the end of the year some 70,000 children were enrolled in primary schools. There was also strong recovery in livestock exports to the Gulf,[30] especially from the north-west.

With the dire humanitarian needs essentially met, the rehabilitation of economic and social infrastructures became the principal focus of the mission. UNOSOM II therefore proposed to set the stage for longer-term development in 1993 through:

- continuing emergency relief operations with a targeted focus;

- the resettlement of refugees and internally-displaced persons;

- the reinvigoration of leading productive sectors in the economy – in particular agriculture, livestock and fisheries – by removing bottlenecks to the expansion of output;

- the revitalization of services, particularly health, water, sanitation and schools; and

- the resuscitation of internal and external commerce and trade.[31]

In the north-west, a modest investment of around US$300,000 was sufficient to facilitate the export of livestock to the Gulf countries through the repair of four culverts along the Bura-Berbera road, the reconstruction of marshalling yards and holding ground, and the provision of veterinary services for the port of Berbera, although UNOSOM II was not able to provide the necessary funds for this purpose. The expansion of livestock exports during the second half of 1993 into 1994 contributed to the growth of economic activity in the region. Economic growth, in turn, enabled the absorption of demobilized militia and returnees into society. In the Benadir region UN agency assistance enabled the port of Mogadishu to be operational for commercial purposes and facilitated the resurgence of exports to the Gulf, Kenya and Europe during the first half of 1994.

Conclusion

The focus of the international community's attention on Somalia was prompted by the tragic humanitarian conditions that existed in 1991–92, which were caused by a long period of internal conflict and drought. The success of the international intervention by the end of 1992 and the beginning of 1993 shifted the focus towards assisting the Somalis to rebuild their political and administrative institutions, and their capacity to develop economically and socially – in short, peacebuilding. The UNOSOM II mandate was designed to achieve this lofty goal.

However, despite the commonality between the Somalis and UNOSOM II with regard to general objectives, UNOSOM II failed to undertake the necessary consultations with the Somalis regarding the specific components of these objectives and the approach to be adopted in the implementation of programmes. Such consultations were necessary to synchronize the efforts of the international community with those to be undertaken by the Somalis themselves. This was particularly important, not only to iron out differences in the interpretation of how to implement an agreement, but also, more fundamentally, to allow the international community and the Somalis to collaborate in tailoring an approach that would take into account historic clan-based divisions. However, this clearly implied that the Somalis needed to agree at the outset – through genuine reconciliation – on what they were collectively prepared to do.

The international community could not impose a solution on the Somalis, even if its objectives were consistent with the Somalis' needs. To reach genuine reconciliation and substantial, if not complete, agreement between Somalis and the international community would have required time and patience and it is well-known why time and patience were lacking during the first quarter of 1993. This lack of patience resulted in the hasty replacement of UNITAF by UNOSOM II, despite the vast differences in the mandates of the two missions. One consequence of this hastiness was the lack of comprehensive and integrated planning in UNOSOM II, a deficiency that became evident when peacebuilding measures were implemented.[32]

In addition, close consultations between the Somalis and the international community would have enabled the parties to understand each other's limitations and thus avoid unrealistic agreements. The Somali declaration of 15 January 1993, for example, that stated that the disarmament process, 'shall commence immediately and be completed in March 1993', which was made without the agreement of UNITAF/UNOSOM, only raised false hopes among Somalis and those who did not know the limitations of UNOSOM I and II. Furthermore, the Addis Ababa Agreement assumed that UNITAF/UNOSOM II would be able to assist in the disarmament process that was to last 90 days from the end of March 1993. These were unrealistic expectations in view of the refusal of UNITAF to take up the task of disarming the Somalis and the unreadiness of UNOSOM II to do so at that time.

Mutual understandings are important for yet another reason – if any Somali group were to deviate from an agreement it could truly be held accountable for not fulfilling its commitment to the agreement. If a party were to remain recalcitrant after being provided with ample opportunity to comply, enforcement measures could ultimately be applied in order to compel the party to meet its commitment.

A full understanding with respect to the interpretation of objectives and approach, is also important to enable the international community to fulfil its part of the agreement. Achieving such an understanding would require that those involved in the mediation and negotiation be central decision-makers in the implementation process. The principal actors from the Somali and the international community side should therefore be the same during the peacemaking and peacekeeping phases. In addition, there must be close and continuous consultations between all actors during the implementation period. The need for consultation, at different stages, between the international community and the nationals of the country is paramount for all missions.

Peace, based on inter-group reconciliation, should be ensured before assistance can be provided for the rehabilitation and reconstruction of institutions and infrastructures. Otherwise dwindling international resources will be wasted if fighting resumes, making it more difficult to finance future deserving peacekeeping and peacebuilding missions. Peace therefore is an absolute prerequisite for the implementation of peacebuilding programmes.

In the case of Somalia, events leading to the 5 June 1993 incident show that the reconciliation process culminating in the agreement reached in Addis Ababa in March 1993 was unravelling. As is well known, despite the enforcement powers of UNOSOM II, the outright opposition of some Somali factions made it impossible for the mission to assist in the rebuilding of institutions. This is clear from the above analysis of disarmament, the re-establishment of political and administrative institutions, and the police and justice system.

Furthermore, had there been peace in Somalia as a result of the implementation of the Addis Ababa Agreement, disarmament would have been the indispensable first step to ensure the longer-term prospect of peacebuilding. Somalia can provide useful lessons in effective disarmament. First, coercive disarmament can be effective only if its purpose is to destroy heavy weaponry. The relinquishing of medium and small weapons can be achieved only voluntarily, especially if the militia forces are inhabiting densely populated areas.

Secondly, disarmament without effective enforcement of an arms embargo is self-defeating. In Somalia since neither UNITAF nor UNOSOM II deployed its forces along the borders the enforcement of an arms embargo was based on the expectation that neighbouring countries would prevent weapons from flowing into the country from or through their territories. However, the national interests of some countries, based on geopolitical considerations, make this expectation unrealistic.

Thirdly, the intention of UNOSOM II to disarm only one faction, without a concomitant and systematic attempt to obtain the co-operation of the others to voluntarily disarm, engendered stiff resistance on the part of the SNA. It further revived inter-clan/faction suspicions and reopened wounds, thus weakening further the 'reconciliation' achieved in Addis Ababa in March 1993. Furthermore, disarmament in the central and southern parts of Somalia could not have been expected to succeed without similar disarmament in the north-east and the north-west.

At the same time, disarmament cannot be expected to succeed solely through the co-operation of the faction leaders or the willingness of the fighters to surrender their weapons. Both leaders and fighters have to be provided with the incentive of something better in the future if weapons are surrendered, and this can be achieved only when society has returned to a state of normality. For the leaders this means their inclusion in the political system which will emerge during and after the transition period, and, for the fighters, an expectation of a better and more normal life.

In order to create such incentives the government must be formed under the principle of national unity, rather than 'winner-takes-all', and there must be a comprehensive programme for the reintegration of demobilized fighters. In the reintegration programme, demobilized fighters must be inter-mingled as thoroughly as possible with returning internally-displaced persons and refugees so that together they may rebuild the physical infrastructures of their communities. In addition, a clear understanding by the Somalis of the massive and comprehensive assistance the international community is prepared to afford, including longer-term rehabilitation, reconstruction and development, can provide in the course of a continuous consultation process a powerful inducement for them to meet the commitments they have made in resolving the conflict.

Once peace has been achieved, as the experience in some parts of Somalia has shown, internal and external trade normally expands. Peace also provides the incentives for capital to flow into the country or a region to meet the need to increase production and trade. Furthermore, the increase in income generates economic activities, such as construction, which further contribute to economic growth. This was the clear lesson of the economy of the north-west during the period mid 1993 to mid-1994 when such results were so clearly visible.

The growth of the economy, in turn, enables the absorption of demobilized fighters and returning displaced persons and refugees. Without economic growth the effect of repatriation and resettlement plans, which usually include skills training and other programmes to equip individuals, may be short-lived. Economic growth also provides the newly-established national and local authorities with the resources to perform their vital functions. Finally, in countries where divisions and animosities have developed, the prospect of increasing income and welfare for 'everyone' makes it more feasible for deeper reconciliation to take hold. In other words, without long-lasting peacebuilding efforts, fragile reconciliation and peace, which a successful peacekeeping mission may have been able to foster, could again unravel.

A mission must also be able to co-ordinate the several components in implementing its programmes. This should be the objective of properly executed integrated planning. The military component, if it is the dominant part of the mission in terms of cost, could contribute to the humanitarian repatriation of the internally displaced and refugees, reintegration, and police programmes by providing, for example, security, logistics support and training. Co-ordination among the civilian components, though equally difficult, is also crucial. From Somalia and other experiences, the co-ordinating mechanisms between the mission, UN agencies, donors and NGOs need to be substantially improved in order to enable the international community to provide a long-lasting impact through its peacekeeping and peacebuilding programmes.

In formulating the mandate for the mission, the SC should also provide, through the assessed budget, the resources necessary to meet the objectives set, including the peacebuilding programmes. The lack of resources for the proper and complete establishment of district and regional councils, the Transitional National Council, the police, the judicial and prison systems, disarmament, the demobilization and reintegration of fighters, the repatriation of internally-displaced persons, humanitarian assistance, and the reconstruction of economic and social infrastructures could only result in failure of the mission. If member states, collectively, are not prepared to fund a programme, the SC should not include it within the mandate of the mission. Otherwise this is a sure way of contributing to the credibility problem of the UN on the ground. But peacekeeping needs sustained peacebuilding components, and all these require a broad mandate and generous resources.

Today Somalia is still in flames, despite the billions of dollars spent to assist in the restoration of institutions and infrastructures, and many of the achievements of the international community may have been undone. After the departure of UNOSOM II the Somali leaders still have not found it possible to work collectively to rebuild their country. If they do, however, it is to be hoped that the international community will learn from past experience and be willing to assist that country once again to become a, 'proud, functioning and viable member of the community of nations'.[33]

NOTES

1. Boutros Boutros-Ghali, *An Agenda for Peace*, New York: United Nations, 1992, para.15, 21.
2. United Nations, *The United Nations and Somalia, 1992–1996*, New York: Department of Public Information, 1996, para.107.
3. Ibid., para.7, 8.
4. UN Security Council Res. 814 (1993), 26 Mar. 1993.
5. United Nations (n.2), para.126.
6. UN Security Council (n.4), section A, para.4(e).
7. UN Doc. S/1994/12, *Further report of the Secretary-General submitted in pursuance of resolution 886 (1993)*, 6 Jan. 1994, para.9, 13.
8. The establishment of the Somali National Consultative Council (SNCC), a consultative body to UNOSOM II, was to be put into effect as soon as a majority of the membership of the Transitional National Council had been nominated by the regional councils and political factions. It was to serve as an advisory body on major national and regional issues. This function would cease immediately after the convening of the Transitional National Council. See: UN Doc. S/26738, *Further report of the Secretary-General submitted in pursuance of paragraph 19 of resolution 814 (1993) and paragraph 5 of resolution 865 (1993)*, 12 Nov. 1993, para.28.
9. The 30 Mar. Agreement, concluded by the same 15 Somali groups whose leaders signed the 27 Mar. Agreement, gave the leading, almost exclusive role in the reconstitution of Somalia's political institutions to those political movements. UN Doc. *Report of the Commission of Inquiry established pursuant to Security Council resolution 885 (1993) to investigate armed attacks on UNOSOM II personnel which led to casualties among them*, para.207.
   The Commission stated further that the 30 Mar. 1993 Agreement went against the: 'letter and spirit of the Agreement of 27 March by stipulating that the names of the three TNC members to be chosen from each district [author's note: should be 'regions'] would be submitted by the political factions [and] the 30 March document made no mention of any reservation of seats for women. It stipulated a 45-day time-frame for the nomination of TNC members, a deadline which gave insufficient time to organize genuine elections at district council level.'
   It concluded that although it bore the signatures of the same leaders who had signed the Agreement of 27 Mar., UNOSOM II never embraced the 30 Mar. document and the stage was set for clashes between UNOSOM II and some of the Somali political groups. Ibid., para.61–3.
10. UN Doc. (n.8), para.27.
11. UN Doc. (n.7), para.9.
12. UN Doc. S/26317, *Further report of the Secretary-General submitted in pursuance of*

paragraph 18 of resolution 814 (1993), 17 Aug. 1993, Annexe I.

13. UN Doc. S/25354, *Further report of the Secretary-General submitted in pursuance of paragraphs 18 and 19 of resolution 792 (1992)*, 3 Mar. 1993, para.86.
14. UN Security Council Res. 865 (1993), 22 Sept. 1993, para.9, 12, 13.
15. UN Doc. (n.12), Annexe I, para.15.
16. UN Doc. S/1995/231, *Report of the Secretary-General on the situation in Somalia submitted in pursuance of paragraph 13 of Security Council resolution 954 (1994)*, 28 Mar. 1995, para.42-4; and UN Doc. S/1994/839, *Further report of the Secretary-General on UNOSOM II submitted in pursuance of paragraph 2 of Security Council resolution 923 (1994)*, 18 July 1994, para.36.
17. However, security could be adversely affected by the divisions between sub-clans and 'sub-sub'clans.
18. UN Doc. (n.12), Annexe I, para.29, 32, 33, 34, 35, 38.
19. UN Doc. (n.9), para.64–9.
20. UN Doc. (n.16), para.46, 47.
21. UN Doc., *Agreement on implementing the cease-fire and on modalities of disarmament*, 15 Jan. 1993, para.1.1, 1.2.
22. UN Doc. (n.13), para.61, 62, 63, 65.
23. UN Doc. A/48/504, *Report of the Secretary-General on emergency assistance for humanitarian relief and the economic and social rehabilitation of Somalia*, 29 Oct. 1993, para.25.
24. UN Doc. A/47/553, *Report of the Secretary-General on emergency assistance for humanitarian relief and the economic and social rehabilitation of Somalia*, 22 Oct. 1992, para.93.
25. UN Doc. A/50/447, *Report of the Secretary-General on assistance for humanitarian relief and the economic and social rehabilitation of Somalia*, 19 Sept. 1995, para.28.
26. Ibid., para.30 and UN Doc. A/49/456, *Report of the Secretary-General concerning assistance for humanitarian relief and the economic and social rehabilitation of Somalia*, 30 Sept. 1994, para.20.
27. This new policy was based on the principle of using only Somali de-miners, according to the UN:

> Recent experience shows that expatriate de-mining firms are not necessarily acceptable to local political authorities and a disproportionate amount of the fees is used to cover the security risks faced by the expatriates. Owing to the employment of the Somali de-miners, many of whom know where the mines are located and who enjoy the support of the local councils or authorities, larger areas have become more accessible for de-mining. It is to be noted that, before any de-mining project is supported, the local de-mining NGO has to satisfy UNOSOM with documentary evidence that the local authorities have agreed that the project can be executed effectively and in reasonable safety within their community. UNOSOM also carries out field survey of the project to ensure its viability. Periodic inspections are carried out during the project implementation to ensure satisfactory completion.

UN Doc. S/1994/614, *Further report of the Secretary-General on UNOSOM, submitted in pursuance of paragraph 14 of resolution 897(1994)*, 24 May 1994, para.53.
28. It was noteworthy that when the reconciliation talks between factions were not faring well, between the Habr Gdir/SNA faction in Galgadud and the Marehan/SNF faction in Abud Waak, for example, no NGO wanted to de-mine areas blocking access to Abud Waak.
29. UN Doc. (n.24), para.3.
30. United Nations (n.2), para.161–2.
31. UN Doc. (n.12), para.50.
32. This, and the lack of co-ordination, are discussed in: Lessons Learned Unit, Department of Peace-keeping Operations, *Comprehensive Report on Lessons-learned from United Nations Operations in Somalia, April 1992–March 1995*, New York: United Nations, Dec. 1995, para.15–31.
33. United Nations (n.2), p.5.

The UN in Mozambique and Angola: Lessons Learned

ASSIS MALAQUIAS

The outcomes of recent peace-building efforts in Africa – often a relapse into war, not sustainable peace – have led to much debate about the internal and external dimensions and factors that determine either success or failure in a peace-building mission. The internal aspects often revolve around the ability to reach a consensus on how to share both political and economic power. However, increasingly the viability of most peace-building efforts in Africa and elsewhere depend on external involvement. Thus the United Nations is regularly called upon to help to draft and implement peace accords. In both Angola and Mozambique the UN was expected to help to create the conditions for sustainable peace. Lack of a consensus at the internal level coupled with an unrealistic UN mandate and the allocation of meagre resources combined to abort the process of peace-building in Angola. In contrast, the successful outcome of the UN mission in Mozambique reflected a much greater international and regional engagement.

The UN's record in peace-building in Africa has been inconsistent, ranging from complete failures to widely celebrated success stories. This article assesses UN attempts to end the cycles of violence and destruction in Angola and Mozambique. Its main objective is to highlight some important lessons to be learned. The article first draws attention to the fact that the peace accords in both countries were designed to end bloody and protracted proxy wars – the twin legacies of Cold War and apartheid destabilization. However, and especially for Angola, the peace accord did not represent a resolution of the main underlying internal problems. The civil war in Angola involved not only high political stakes, but even greater economic interests given the country's immense natural resources. Lack of a consensus on how Angola's wealth should be divided in a post-conflict era ultimately booby-trapped the entire peace-building operation. Political consensus in Mozambique would have been easier to achieve if the resource issue had been absent.

Secondly, the article suggests that the different outcomes of the UN efforts in Angola and in Mozambique reflect the level of international commitment and engagement mobilized. Inability, or unwillingness, to

Assis Malaquias is Assistant Professor, Department of Government at St. Lawrence University in Canton, NY.

commit enough resources to support peace-building efforts in Angola ultimately rendered the entire UN operation ineffective. The UN Angola Verification Mission (UNAVEM II) simply did not have the mandate, nor the means, to deal forcefully with any spoilers' attempts to derail the implementation of the peace accord. In contrast, in Mozambique – despite some problems related to the demobilization of soldiers – the commitment of adequate resources, together with active/dynamic international involvement ultimately guaranteed success.

Thirdly, the article highlights some important lessons from the UN's experience in Angola and Mozambique. The contrasting results in the two cases show the importance of realistic mandates, coupled with adequate commitment of resources. In Angola the mandate to monitor and verify was unsuitable for such a complex situation. Further, the allocation of meagre resources to carry out such a mandate also contributed to its failure. In Mozambique the UN's direct and dynamic involvement, together with adequate human and material resources, decisively contributed to success.

Another important lesson relates to the types of structure designed to support peace-building efforts. In the case of Angola the main structure upon which the entire operation was based was rigid and ineffective. Again, this starkly contrasts with the experience in Mozambique, where the UN had a central role in all aspects of peace-building. Finally, the most important lesson to be learnt relates to the need to create unified, professional armed forces well ahead of elections. Failure to do so in Angola eased the relapse into war.

The article concludes by suggesting that the UN must take a more long-term approach to peace-building. It must be viewed as a critical component of a process that also involves enhancing governance and reconstituting civil society as a first step to reversing the political, administrative and economic decay that has caused so much human misery in Africa and elsewhere.

Historical Contexts

The collapse of the Portuguese colonial regime in 1974[1] precipitated profound transformations in southern Africa that eventually led to processes of democratic transition in Namibia, Zimbabwe and South Africa. Ironically, the former Portuguese colonies in the region – Angola and Mozambique – have not fared nearly as well. By the early 1990s long years of civil war coupled with economic mismanagement and widespread corruption had brought these two countries to the anarchical stage that Kaplan referred to in his celebrated article.[2] Both Angola and Mozambique were on the verge of joining the growing list of collapsed states in Africa.

Important domestic, regional and international factors were threatening the viability of these new and fragile states. The departure of the settler communities and subsequent mismanagement had driven their economies to ruin; civil war had paralysed already weak states, rendering them inoperative in terms of their reach and authority outside the state capitals and a handful of major cities and resulting in their incapacity to provide security – let alone law and order – to their citizens. Further, the authority of the state in both Angola and Mozambique was being further challenged by two powerful armed groups: Uniao Nacional para a Independencia Total de Angola (UNITA) and Resistencia Nacional Mocambicana (RENAMO) that ruled over a large, populated portion of the country and that had a working political-military apparatus and an organized economy, albeit a primitive one.

By the early 1990s, the survival of the state in both Angola and Mozambique demanded an end to the civil wars and the establishment of an open, multiparty political system, as a first step in a comprehensive process of state reconstitution. Thus, on 31 May 1991, the Angolan government and UNITA reached a wide-ranging peace accord in Bicesse, Portugal, that was expected to pave the way for a peaceful transition to an elected government and democratic development. Likewise, on 4 October 1992, Mozambique's government and RENAMO signed a similar agreement in Rome. Given the fragility of the state in these two former colonies, the UN was expected to facilitate both transition processes through peacekeeping.

Although Angola and Mozambique share important similarities in terms of historical experience – both achieved independence from Portugal after protracted wars of national liberation and are governed by Marxist liberation movements – their transition to peace and elected governments produced different outcomes. Angola's aborted transition did not end the cycle of war, while Mozambique, in spite of some serious problems, described below, has succeeded in ending the war and has put in place the basis for democratic development centred around a vibrant parliament and enriched by a re-emergent civil society.

Peace-building in Angola and Mozambique: Domestic and International Constraints

On 29 and 30 September 1992 Angola held its first multiparty, internationally-supervised elections. The governing Movimento Popular de Libertacao de Angola (MPLA) won a parliamentary majority of 53.7 per cent, compared to 34.1 for UNITA. In the presidential elections the incumbent, José Eduardo dos Santos, won 49.7 per cent of the vote to Jonas Savimbi's 40.1, just 0.6 per cent short of the 50 needed to avert a run-off presidential election. UNITA rejected the validity of the results, which were sanctioned by the UN and other international observers, declaring that massive fraud had taken place. Simultaneously, it militarily occupied large portions of the country and, in a gambit reminiscent of events following independence in 1975, attempted to take the capital city. Fighting for control of Luanda began on 30 October. After several days of intense fighting the government prevailed. Several senior UNITA officials, including its vice-president Jeremias Chitunda, were killed. Another peace process had collapsed and, once again, Angola reverted to full-scale civil war.

While the UN was attempting to end the new round of bloodletting in Angola, it was also involved in a more peaceful mission in Mozambique. There, on 27 to 29 October 1994, 90 per cent of the 6.4 million registered voters cast their ballots in the first ever presidential and legislative elections.[3] In the presidential election, the incumbent, President Joaquim Chissano, polled 53.3 per cent to 33.7 for the RENAMO leader Afonso Dhlakama. FRELIMO won the legislative election with 44.3 per cent, followed by RENAMO with 37.8.

Despite maintaining that there were serious irregularities in the electoral process, Dhlakama telephoned the UN Secretary-General Boutros Boutros-Ghali to accept the outcome that had been certified as free and fair by the UN Operation in Mozambique (ONUMOZ) and more than 2,300 international observers. By accepting the election results, Dhlakama was quashing insistent rumours that he would take his organization back to the jungle, as Savimbi had done in Angola. In the end, Dhlakama accepted the results while insisting that, 'the elections were not free and fair.'[4]

With RENAMO committed to play a peaceful role as FRELIMO's opposition in parliament, ONUMOZ, at a cost of nearly US$1 billion, could be declared a success and its 5,500 peacekeepers were withdrawn gradually. By the time the newly elected government took office in December 1994, only a small contingent of peacekeepers remained in Mozambique to provide mine-clearance training.

At about the same time that the international community was celebrating another success story in UN peacekeeping and peace-building in Mozambique, the two warring factions in Angola were reaching yet another peace accord under UN auspices to pave the way for a government of national unity.[5] At the time of writing, there is justified scepticism about this new accord's chances of finally ending the vicious cycle of war in Angola. As the UN embarks on a renewed peacekeeping effort there, it is important to identify the factors that accounted for the differing outcomes in the attempts to end the wars and set both countries on a course towards peaceful and democratic development.

At the domestic level in Angola, the two factions could find agreement only on how to restructure the political system. They were far apart on the more important question of how to share the country's wealth, especially its oil and diamond revenues.[6] By the time the peace accord was signed, the government controlled the oil-producing regions in Cabinda, Zaire and Kwanza Norte, while UNITA controlled most of the diamond mining in the Lunda Norte and Lunda Sul. UNITA was simply not ready to give the diamond-producing areas over to the governing MPLA, especially since it regarded the government as corrupt. Thus UNITA demanded its participation in the management of the funds accruing from the sale of oil and diamonds in order to prevent the continuing enrichment of the MPLA. The Angolan government's inability to address important domestic problems – including corruption, economic mismanagement and the uneven distribution of wealth – ultimately contributed to the breakdown of the entire peace process. UNITA preferred to continue exploiting the diamond areas it controlled – instead of being completely co-opted into the government and ruling party – unless it had guarantees of its fair share of the country's wealth.

At the international level, the UN failed to engage sufficient resources to compel the two factions to abide by the Bicesse accord they had signed in May 1991. Ironically, the end of the Cold War, in which Angola had played a conspicuous part, at least in terms of superpower rivalry in southern Africa, did not benefit the country. In fact, it may be argued that the end of bipolarity and the dawn of a new era of co-operation revolving around the UN and other international organizations produced a new set of pressures and demands, including a scarcity of international resources for peace-building and peacekeeping. Now Angola had to compete with other countries, such as Cambodia, El Salvador and Mozambique, for both attention and resources. As a result, the international community, and particularly the United States and Russia, were not as willing to employ the same resources to make peace in Angola in the 1990s as they had to make war in the 1970s and the 1980s. In the end the adversaries in Angola kept their armies intact, making a return to war inevitable.

Mozambique did not have the same domestic or international problems. Without valuable resources such as oil or diamonds to fight over, RENAMO resorted to demanding financial help from the international community. Western pledges of money helped to induce Afonso Dhlakama to sign the peace accord. The international community, particularly the United States and South Africa, contributed considerable financial resources toward the establishment of a trust fund to help to finance RENAMO's transformation into a political party. Arguably, however, the most important factor in explaining the success, or lack of it, in both UN missions relates to the allocation of resources.

UNAVEM: Peacekeeping 'On the Cheap'

Both the Bicesse and the Rome accord were expected to be the first steps in comprehensive, protracted and multi-layered processes of transition to elected, democratic governments in Angola and Mozambique. The accords included: provisions for a cease-fire; the fundamental principles for peace; the main concepts for the resolution of outstanding questions between the warring parties; electoral and internal security provisions for the transition period to elections; administrative structures; and arrangements for the creation of unified armed forces. But the main difference between the two accords resided in the nature and the level of UN involvement. Whereas in Angola the accord had a major and fatal flaw – it failed to establish the framework for a strong UN involvement capable of providing both protection and guarantees strong enough to force strict compliance with the accord – in Mozambique the entire transition process was based on a strong and activist UN engagement.

UNAVEM had not been created to enforce the implementation of the Bicesse accord. It was created on 20 December 1988 to monitor the withdrawal of the 50,000-strong Cuban military contingent from Angola, as part of the settlement that led to Namibia's independence. This mission was made up of 70 military observers and 20 civilian officials from ten countries[7] and was given a 31-month mandate, beginning with its deployment one week before the start of the Cuban withdrawal and ending one month after its completion.

On the eve of the signing of the Bicesse accord, the UN Security Council (SC) agreed to extend UNAVEM's mandate. UNAVEM II would become a 24-nation multinational force with the mission of monitoring the cease-fire between the Angolan government and UNITA. A budget of US$132.3 million dollars and 548 personnel were allocated for it, which began its deployment on 1 July 1991.[8]

UN personnel comprised 350 military observers and 90 police officers. The military observers were given the task of ensuring that the provisions of the peace accord, regarding the encampment of government troops in 27 zones and UNITA in 23 other zones, were respected. They were also deployed in 12 critical areas and had additional responsibilities for conducting patrols over the entire country. UNAVEM II also included 90 international police officers whose main task was to ensure the functioning of a new, integrated national police force.

On 24 March 1992 the SC unanimously approved the expansion of UNAVEM II and the enlargement of its mandate. A 400-strong division was added to the existing mission to monitor and evaluate the operations and impartiality of the electoral authorities at all levels in the legislative and presidential elections. This division was expected to operate in all 18 provinces to monitor and verify the three main phases of the electoral process, including the registration of voters, the electoral campaign and the poll itself. An additional US$18.8 million was allocated to UNAVEM II's budget for these purposes.[9]

In terms of both human and financial resources, UNAVEM II was, at best, a diminutive reproduction of other UN operations, such as in Namibia and Cambodia. In contrast to the UN role during Namibia's transition to independence, UNAVEM II did not organize the elections. The UN stressed that the Angolan elections were essentially a national, sovereign affair. Therefore the UN assumed an auxiliary role – to observe and verify the elections, not to organize them. As the Secretary-General emphasized:

> the government must be seen clearly to be taking charge of their organization, especially concerning logistics.[10]

This was expected of a country emerging from a devastating civil war that had crippled most of its infrastructure. By contrast, in Namibia – a country of roughly one million people with most of its infrastructure and bureaucracy intact – the UN mounted a full-scale operation involving more than 6,000 personnel.

This stance by the UN was partly responsible for a transition process fraught with fear and tension. The UN did not intervene in preventing armed UNITA cadres in civilian clothing from moving into towns across the country. Nor did it investigate widespread reports by frightened local people of UNITA arms caches. Moreover, UNITA's heavy arms were not brought into the internationally-supervised cantonments of troops, as the peace accord required.

Not surprisingly, UNAVEM II was not able to defuse escalating tension ahead of the country's first multi-party elections and was caught completely unprepared to deal with pre-electoral clashes between the former warring parties.

The failure to steer the peace process and the transition to elected government and a democratic regime in Angola was, to a considerable degree, a failure of the UN. This derived from the mismatch between the role of the UN mission in Angola and the realities of the Angolan conflict. The stated goal of the UN mission in Angola was neither peace-building, peacemaking, peacekeeping nor peace enforcement. It was vaguely defined as verification and monitoring.

Consequently, the UN force was unable to act as a deterrent, nor was the UN effective in: reconstituting/reducing the two armies; creating a new police force; reforming the judicial and electoral systems; instigating human rights; or land reform. The difficulties inherent in a post-civil war society, compounded by Angola's weak bureaucracy and the profound distrust between the MPLA and UNITA, had left vital features of the transition process unfulfilled, in particular the demobilization of the two armies and their fusion into a single, unified, non-partisan, national army. These difficulties impeded the government in carrying out some of the basic functions required during an election, such as the efficient distribution and collection of ballot boxes.

Given its limited resources, the UN mission was also unable to make a definitive pronouncement on whether the exercise had been free and fair in a manner that could satisfy all parties. In the end, given all of these shortcomings, the UN was not able to prevent the reversion to war.

Ultimately, the failure of the mission in Angola must be evaluated within the context of the expanded role that the UN took on in the post-Cold War international environment. The UN's new interventionism induced severe budgetary strains that were not always mitigated by member countries, who faced their own internal problems of adjusting to new circumstances. The post-Cold War situation also consolidated American and Western domination within the UN. The UN could be mobilized to act decisively and forcefully in the Gulf to defend Western interests but – symptomatic of Africa's marginalization – not in Angola. Here the UN was relegated to an essentially secondary role. However, as outlined below, a more central role for the UN in Mozambique produced a better outcome, despite some difficulties.

ONUMOZ: A Success Story

The UN involvement in Mozambique reflected a desire not to repeat the blunders made in Angola. Thus shortly after the signing of the peace agreement in Rome, the UN General Assembly (GA) approved a budget of US$140 million to finance the initial phase of ONUMOZ and the first steps were taken to deploy the 5,500 peacekeepers mandated to oversee the application of the agreement.

Another key factor in explaining the success of ONUMOZ resides in the fact that the UN insisted on the establishment of flexible mechanisms to help to carry out the peace accord. In Angola the entire process was supervised by the Joint Political-Military Commission (JPMC) made up of government and UNITA representatives, while the UN, along with the United States, Russia and Portugal sat in as observers. However, in contrast, ONUMOZ worked with many commissions created specifically to ease the implementation of the peace agreement. These commissions invariably included members of the FRELIMO government, RENAMO and ONUMOZ. ONUMOZ, for example, was an integral part of two key commissions: the

Supervision and Control Commission that held primary responsibility for the day-to-day management of the transition process and the Cease-Fire Commission that dealt with incidents and complaints from either side. It also played an important role in the National Electoral Commission, territorial administration, information and police affairs.

Arguably, however, the success of ONUMOZ rested largely on its leadership role in the Commission for the Formation of the Armed Forces. The UN had the primary responsibility for managing the encampment and registration of up to 100,000 government and RENAMO soldiers. The UN was also responsible for ensuring that a new national army of 30,000 was created with equal numbers drawn from the government and RENAMO forces before elections took place.

ONUMOZ established 150 assembly areas, where soldiers were gathered and registered. An important screening process then took place with some soldiers being selected to join the new armed forces while others were offered the opportunity to participate in a social adjustment programme devised by the UN to help demobilized soldiers adapt to civilian life. Some soldiers opted to go back immediately to their places of origin. However, many others participated in various technical courses offered by the UN to ease their return to civilian life.

By the end of March 1994 nearly 50,000 troops had been confined in UN cantonment sites. Many camps were already full and some had more than double the forces they were initially supposed to hold. Since the process had gone according to plan, ONUMOZ could concentrate on the establishment of a new army. The tragic situation in Angola had taught the UN that the formation of a national army before the elections was a basic condition for the peace process to succeed. In Angola the UN could not concentrate on the creation of a new, unified army, partly owing to its secondary role in the JPMC. It was able only hastily to proclaim the existence of a single armed force and the disbanding of troops a few days before the elections were held. In reality, both the MPLA and UNITA kept their crack units in place as a precaution. What followed was an armed conflict even more serious than the previous ones, with the warring factions emerging on the ground better equipped than ever before.

The UN was determined not to repeat the mistake in Mozambique. Thus several military centres for the new army were created to provide both training and the possibility of former combatants developing mutual trust. ONUMOZ also ensured that, as the soldiers presented themselves for registration, a distribution of food and clothing accompanied the process of disarmament and the collection of war material; and when possible, that there was social and medical assistance available to their dependents.

The UN had to exert great pressure on both the Mozambique

government and RENAMO to commit themselves to a final date to end demobilization. There was some speculation that the government, in particular, was deliberately keeping back many of its best troops from the disarmament process. A major snag developed over the case of what became known as the 'missing 12,000 FRELIMO troops'. More than 18 months after the signing of the peace accord, the government claimed that its army was in fact some 12,000 smaller than previously believed. Predictably, RENAMO was not impressed with this government 'miscounting', believing that FRELIMO had been massaging the figures to hide soldiers.[11]

But RENAMO was causing its own set of problems. FRELIMO complained, for example, that RENAMO was confining mostly children, elderly and disabled people in assembly areas, while hiding its best soldiers.[12] FRELIMO also observed, with concern, that the weapons delivered by RENAMO to ONUMOZ were not only old and obsolete but did not correspond to the principle of one man, one weapon. In other words, RENAMO was allegedly hiding away its most sophisticated weapons. Furthermore and in open contradiction of the General Peace Agreement and its own public statements, RENAMO was allegedly continuing to ban the movement of citizens in areas under its control through arbitrary detention and intimidation.

Given the long history of animosity between the former warring factions, the mutual accusations that dominated the transition process were expected even in the most optimistic scenarios. What was not envisaged was that ONUMOZ successes would create difficulties. One of the main problems arose from the fact that, having encamped most of the government and RENAMO soldiers, ONUMOZ was unable to demobilize them quickly enough. As a result, many soldiers became involved in mutinies and other disturbances, because they wanted to know whether they would be demobilized or whether they would join the new national army.

In the Boane and Moamba assembly areas, for example, soldiers rioted and seized several UN personnel and their vehicles. They moved outside the camp and sacked shops, beat people and caused UN personnel to flee from the assembly area. In a worrying development, former combatants in other assembly areas began to adopt similar tactics. Once they heard how their colleagues elsewhere had been able to secure immediate demobilization by seizing hostages or through another favourite tactic – blocking a major road for a day or two – riots quickly spread to other camps. Although no UN personnel were seriously hurt, FRELIMO and RENAMO commanders were regularly beaten up, innocent civilians were killed, raped or saw their property looted.

In one incident mutinying soldiers of the 6th Tank Brigade returned to their barracks in a suburb of Maputo only after holding talks with the Chief of the General Staff of the Mozambique Armed Forces. In this frightening episode the Mozambique government blamed ONUMOZ for not deactivating the tanks used by the mutinying soldiers. However, the UN claimed that the government did not allow ONUMOZ to make the tanks inoperable by removing firing mechanisms. In the end, ONUMOZ was able to put the entire process quickly back on track.

The nature and level of UN involvement in Mozambique's transition process also helped to diffuse a potentially catastrophic pre-electoral crisis. One day before Mozambicans were expected to go to the polls, RENAMO pulled out of the electoral process claiming to have uncovered a number of irregularities that endangered the whole process. These allegedly included:

> a lack of timely presentation and verification of all surplus voter registration and voting material; the fact that voting booth lists were not handed over to the Elections Administration Technical Secretariat, all leaders and the political parties; and the fact that voter lists had not been put up at the voting places.[13]

In an ominous move, Dhlakama declared, like Savimbi in Angola, that he would not accept the result if RENAMO lost.[14] But, unlike in Angola, ONUMOZ was quickly able to convince Dhlakama that his actions would not be tolerated by the international community. The Front Line States, in particular, threatened strong measures and did not rule out the possibility of swift military action if RENAMO resumed the war. Dhlakama had no choice but to quickly rejoin the electoral process. In a face-saving statement, he declared that:

> the international community gave us guarantees that irregularities reported by RENAMO will be investigated henceforth and other complaints will be looked into after elections. ... I would like to announce that RENAMO will participate in elections.[15]

This ensured that the elections would take place without any major incident.

With the electoral process completed, the UN could rightly congratulate itself on having achieved another peace-building success. However, even in Mozambique, the UN's work was not complete, particularly as regards weapons collection and mine clearance. Aldo Ajello, the dynamic Special Representative of the Secretary-General in Mozambique, was forced to acknowledge that mine clearance had been one of ONUMOZ's weakest points. According to Ajello, the mine-clearing programme was planned to last two years, but it had to be completed in six months, mainly due to 'administrative problems between New York and Maputo'.[16]

Moreover, lack of confidence between the two parties made them reluctant to indicate the locations of minefields. This means that, although the war has ended, innocent victims will continue to be killed and maimed for years, perhaps decades to come.

What lessons, then, can be derived from the UN's experiences in Angola and Mozambique? The UN's efforts in peace-building and peacekeeping in these two countries demonstrate that a clear mandate, functional transitional institutions and emphasis on the creation of a unified army well ahead of elections are crucial factors in determining success or failure.

The Importance of Realistic Mandates

One of the main differences between the UN missions in Angola and Mozambique may be found in the resources allocated to UNAVEM II and ONUMOZ, respectively. However, although severely constrained by a lack of resources, UNAVEM II could have done a much better job if it had been given a more realistic mandate. Its weak mandate reflected the UN's general practice of not challenging the sovereignty of member states. However, as mentioned before, Angola's long years of civil war and economic mismanagement had brought the country to the verge of total collapse. Given this situation, a more realistic mandate for UNAVEM II would have included measures to facilitate state reconstitution concurrently with the peace process. This could have involved the restoration of state authority in areas still controlled by UNITA. Failure to do so emboldened UNITA which, predictably, undertook to undermine the power of the MPLA regime during the transition process through an intense campaign of intimidation and political violence.

The peace accord rested on the crucial assumption that both sides would co-operate in its implementation, since, at least outwardly, all wanted peace. Instead, UNITA took full advantage of the prevailing situation – a weak government, a dysfunctional JPMC and an ineffective UNAVEM II – to strengthen its own position, partly by preventing the government from extending its administration to areas it had lost during the civil war.

Ironically, the UN unwittingly aided UNITA's attempts to keep tens of thousands of peasants under its control – instead of allowing them to return to their villages under the terms of the peace accord – because of the substantial quantities of food aid supplied to the area by UN agencies for distribution by UNITA officials.[17] This reflected a lack of UN 'intelligence' regarding the domestic political situation.

But there were other factors contributing to political violence. Contrary to what happened in Mozambique, the demobilized soldiers from both armies in Angola retained many of their weapons because of the haphazard way in which the demobilization process was conducted, again reflecting a lack of proper UNAVEM II involvement. In many cases soldiers simply did not report back to their barracks once the cease-fire was signed. There were credible reports of 'tens of thousands of angry and penniless FAPLA soldiers' stopping traffic and rushing on to aircraft in an attempt to return to their homes.[18] Only 38 per cent of FAPLA soldiers were officially demobilized; the rest simply abandoned their units and looked for the fastest way home.[19] During the long journey back home, most of these former soldiers resorted to criminal activities to survive.

The government's inability to handle increasing political violence in the period leading up to elections was related to the fact that, paradoxically, peace had eroded its power by transferring authority to new structures such as the JPMC, but these proved to be highly dysfunctional. Moreover, the three powers expected to act as the guarantors of peace in Angola were not prepared to employ extraordinary measures, such as the use of military force, to enforce the peace agreements. All these factors contributed to a situation of uncertainty that escalated into hostility and political violence that, ultimately, brought down the entire process. Thus the first multiparty elections in Angola amounted to little more than 'an exercise in make-believe'.[20] When the elections were held, many of the fundamental preconditions stipulated in the peace accord remained unfulfilled. The accord had failed to create a peaceful climate for political discourse. The two main opponents – having been denied victory on the battlefield – were attempting to win the civil war at the ballot box. Both sides still had armies and UNITA still controlled the territory it occupied during the war.

The worst fears were realized when, after the publication of the election results, Savimbi ordered his army back to war. Savimbi was not stopped, partly because the structures designed to manage the transition process proved to be highly dysfunctional and partly because a unified army had not yet been created.

Managing Transitions: The Importance of Functional Structures

The primary responsibility for implementing the peace accord in Angola, unlike Mozambique, did not rest with the UN, but with a joint political-military commission, the JPMC. Predictably, this structure was incapable of managing a peaceful transition to the elections. In fact, it was not even able to prevent the peace process from beginning to unravel soon after the signing of the accord in Portugal.

UNITA withdrew from this joint commission in the early stages of its existence, claiming that the MPLA government was not seriously implementing the accord and was thus endangering the entire peace process. Although UNITA returned to the JPMC shortly afterwards, this body had lost much of its effectiveness. Without a strong mechanism to manage the transition process the country completed its descent into political turmoil, characterized by intimidation and violence. As a crucial mechanism for the transition process, the JPMC was poorly designed because many of the problems it had to face were not anticipated by the signatories of the accord.

The Central Role of a National, Unified Army

Under the Bicesse accord the Angolan government and UNITA were expected to form a new 50,000-strong united army from their estimated 250,000 troops and demobilize the rest before elections were held. However, from the start the process of assembling government and rebel troops was very slow, resulting in huge delays in the establishment of the new army. This slowness was caused by lack of food, transportation and other logistical problems in the areas where the troops should have been confined.

In a report to the SC, the Secretary-General pointed out that two-and-a-half months after the assembling of troops was supposed to have been completed, barely 60 per cent of those declared by both sides had been encamped in assembly areas.[21] The report declared that this state of affairs undermined confidence and imperilled the implementation of other aspects of the accord.[22]

UNITA claimed that it had concluded the process of confining its troops to UN-controlled assembly areas just before the 15 November 1991 deadline stipulated by the JPMC. UNITA noted that not all government troops had been encamped and suggested that many government soldiers were being transferred from the army into the secret police and the Public Order Police to avoid demobilization.[23] According to UNAVEM II's count, a total of 95,634 troops (68,666 government troops and 26,968 from UNITA) were in 45 assembly areas, compared with the projected total of 165,440 that should have been in the assembly areas in their totality (115,640 government troops and 49,800 from UNITA).[24]

By early April 1992 it became clear that the provisions of the peace accord regarding the formation of a unified national army would not be met. Given the slow pace of implementing some of the crucial aspects of the accord, the UN and the foreign powers involved in overseeing the peace process had all but given up attempting to meet the stipulated schedule for demobilizing approximately 250,000 soldiers and guerrillas and forming a unified army before the elections. The British, Portuguese and French officers in charge of forming the new army had succeeded only in creating a unified command structure on paper.[25] Thus in a move that would prove fatal to the country's long-term unity and stability, the parties involved undertook to make the first serious revision of the accord. The government and UNITA decided to hold back on their initial pledge to demobilize all their soldiers or integrate them into the new national army. UNITA decided to keep at least 15,000 soldiers in reserve, while the government kept about 33,000 in reserve, including a 6,000-strong air force and a 4,000-strong navy.

A month before the elections only about 25 per cent of the combined soldiers had been demobilized and a mere 12 per cent of the national army had been formed.[26] It was becoming clear that Angola would not have one army, but three – the embryonic national army, FAPLA and FALA – at election time.

Pressed by the United States, Russia and Portugal, who were the international observers to the peace process, the MPLA government and UNITA agreed to disband their armies officially on 27 September 1992, just 48 hours before the start of the first democratic elections in Angola. However, the unity of the new armed forces, the Angolan Armed Forces (FAA), lasted only a week. UNITA withdrew from the newly-formed joint armed forces on 5 October.

Conclusion

The UN's peace-building and peacekeeping efforts in Angola and Mozambique demonstrate that, in the final analysis, a clear mandate and the commitment of adequate resources are the main determining factors in a mission's success or failure. In Mozambique, ONUMOZ had both a clear mandate and the means to play the pivotal role that is expected of a UN mission. ONUMOZ was given the clear mandate of managing the entire peace process. Further, the sizeable UN presence served both as an incentive for the former enemies fully to implement the peace agreement they had signed and as a credible deterrent against any ploy to re-ignite the civil war.

In Angola, UNAVEM II never had the mandate to manage the implementation of the peace process. Surprisingly, it was relegated to a secondary role. As such, it could not help to solve the country's multifaceted and multi-layered crises before elections took place. The severity of these crises would have required a much longer transition process in order to allow for the bolstering of credible governance and the reconstitution of civil society. In Angola, as in many other African countries, there is a 'crisis of governance'.[27] This is reflected in the 'coercive and arbitrary'[28] nature of the state, where government officials habitually follow their own interests without fear of accountability. In the case of Angola, UNITA believed that, after spending many decades in the jungle, it was now its turn to pillage the country's wealth, as the MPLA government had done in the past.

If the peace process is to work in Angola under UN supervision, the UN

must necessarily take into account this crisis of governance. It must take
steps to remedy political and administrative decay and initiate a process of
political renewal that will ultimately lead to the development of pluralistic
institutions, respect for the rule of law, a free press and the protection of
human rights. This would also entail a working to strengthen elements of
civil society to enable it to play a more significant role in the peace process.
As Angola demonstrates, without civil society's involvement the field is left
almost exclusively to the political parties with powerful military wings.

NOTES

1. On 25 Apr. 1974 a group of Portuguese junior officers dissatisfied with their country's
   colonial policies, including the counter-insurgency wars in Angola, Guinea-Bissau and
   Mozambique, led a military coup that toppled the fascist regime of Marcelo Caetano.
2. Robert Kaplan, 'The Coming Anarchy', *Atlantic Monthly*, Feb. 1994.
3. Presidential Decree 1/94 of 11 Apr. 1994 had set the election dates for 27–28 Oct. 1994.
   However, voting was extended by one day to accommodate RENAMO, which had staged a
   one-day boycott of the elections.
4. Afonso Dhlakama, Radio Mozambique, 14 Nov. 1994.
5. The Angolan government and UNITA signed their latest formal peace accord in Lusaka on
   20 Nov. 1994.
6. Angola earns an average of US$5 billion p.a. from oil and US$1 billion p.a. from diamonds.
7. Algeria, Argentina, Brazil, the Congo, Czechoslovakia, India, Jordan, Norway, Spain and the
   former Yugoslavia.
8. Besides the original participants, 14 other countries also participated, including Canada,
   Egypt, Guinea-Bissau, Hungary, Ireland, Malaysia, Morocco, The Netherlands, New
   Zealand, Nigeria, Senegal, Singapore, Sweden and Zimbabwe.. UNAVEM II personnel
   included 350 military observers, up to 90 police officers, 14 medical staff, 80 international
   and 80 local staff for administrative and support units. The entire operation was supported
   by three aircraft and 12 helicopters (figures taken from a Reuters dispatch from the UN, 31
   May 1991).
9. Reuters, 24 Mar. 1992.
10. Xinhua News Agency, 6 Mar. 1991.
11. BBC World Service (in English), 5 May 1994.
12. Final Communique of the Fourth Session of FRELIMO's Central Committee held in Matola,
    28 Mar. 1994; in *Noticias*, Maputo, 2 Apr. 1994, p.2.
13. Radio Mozambique, 27 Oct. 1994.
14. BBC World Service (in English), 26 Oct. 1994.
15. Radio Mozambique, 28 Oct. 1994.
16. *Le Soir* (Brussels), 18 Nov. 1994, p.2.
17. *Guardian,* 23 Mar. 1992, p.7.
18. Ibid.
19. Ibid.
20. Christine Messiant, Centre d'Etudes Africaines, Paris, quoted in Inter Press Service, 26 Sept.
    1992.
21. Xinhua News Service, 6 Nov. 1991.
22. Ibid.
23. Voice of the Resistance of the Black Cockerel (UNITA's clandestine radio station), 18 Nov.
    1991.
24. *Washington Post,* 11 Apr. 1992, p.A14.
25. Ibid.

26. Inter Press Service, 26 Aug. 1992.
27. World Bank, *Sub-Saharan Africa: from Crisis to Sustainable Growth*, Washington, DC: World Bank, 1989, p.60.
28. Ibid.

HUMANITARIAN AND MILITARY CO-OPERATION

Improving UN Developmental Co-ordination within Peace Missions

J. DAVID WHALEY

The work of the United Nations in development is essential to the success of the UN in its various non-development missions. Most important are the links between development and peace. This article reviews the challenge, indeed the crisis, facing UN peace missions and, above all, their developmental components. In so doing it identifies some critical elements that could constitute an essential agenda for peacebuilding; it suggests some basic principles that would help in the design of more appropriate responses; and it seeks to measure performance against these principles, and to identify mechanisms that would assist in their implementation. Finally, it addresses the complex issue of financing development within peace missions.

In his recent clarion call for sustained support for development co-operation, James Gustave Speth, Administrator of the United Nations Development Programme (UNDP), underlined that:

> the UN's work in development is essential to the success of the UN in its various non-development missions. Most important are the links between development and peace...Degrading poverty, diminishing material resources and increasing joblessness all feed ethnic and social tensions. It is from this cauldron that crises boil over.[1]

Of 82 significant conflicts in the last three years, 79 have been within a nation, not between nations, and 90 per cent of the casualties have been civilians, not soldiers. As Speth comments:

> These conflicts require development upstream, not soldiers downstream...acting preventively, landing development now, instead of peacekeepers tomorrow...If we want a UN for peace, we need a UN for development.[2]

The founding fathers of the UN clearly recognized this, as they struggled to bring to a close half a century of world war. Political leaders, economists and generals alike concluded that an enduring peace would be one founded on expanding prosperity and social justice. The UN was built on a vision of

J. David Whaley is the first Resident Co-ordinator of the Operational Activities for Development of the UN System and Resident Representative of the UNDP in South Africa.

a broader victory – not only over aggression and war but also over want and despair. Only victory on both fronts could assure the world lasting peace. This was duly embodied in the Preamble of the UN Charter itself with its commitment to:

> employ international machinery for the promotion of the economic and social advancement of all its peoples.

Over 50 years later, the justification of the UN and its moral authority is based on the principle that the world body should reflect the priorities of nations. The priority of most people is development. If that is not respected in the activities of the UN, the political compact that holds the world organization together will be likely to crumble.

We have recently commemorated the first half century of the existence of the UN and emerged from the Cold War that frustrated the ambitions of the international community for much of that period. As we enter a new era there is a clear need for a UN that is a strong and effective force for sustainable, people-centred development; that is built as a bulwark for protecting the security of people, and also the security of nations.

The Challenge

Assistance to rebuild war-torn societies, disintegrated states and the shattered economies that generally accompany them is an essential and integral part of the efforts of the international community and the UN to bring about, maintain and consolidate peace. The many armed conflicts, mostly within states, that have broken out since the end of the Cold War pose a threat to peace at local, regional and global levels, thus justifying an increased involvement of the international community in conflict prevention and resolution. Primarily as a result of armed conflicts, millions of people have been compelled to leave their homes; their traditional coping capacities have been destroyed or seriously weakened; and they inevitably find themselves in need of urgent support for their very survival. Demands for conflict-related humanitarian assistance have increased far faster than any other claims on international solidarity in recent years. Yet, despite the growth of resources channelled to humanitarian and emergency relief, this has now resulted both in a 'humanitarian deficit' and in a growing concern over the effectiveness of relief as it is currently provided.

Tragically, funding of the deficit has largely been at the expense of development co-operation. Member states that face a combination of domestic debt, increasing social claims on limited resources and deficit reduction strategies have to make critical choices in taking on the growing burden of their international obligations.

Peacekeeping – the only form of international operations based essentially on assessed contributions – is best protected from domestic budgetary constraints, although challenges to the principle of collective commitment and the late payment of dues are proving a colossal headache. Humanitarian assistance is generally forthcoming, at least for the present, as a result of public pressure, and influenced by the ever-present media that bring human tragedy far more readily into our homes. However, development co-operation, traditionally funded from voluntary governmental contributions, benefits neither from the internationally-agreed nature of peacekeeping funding nor from direct appeals to the public for gestures of solidarity in the face of life-threatening dramas.

The combined costs of peacekeeping operations, humanitarian assistance and what remains of development co-operation, have brought the whole UN system to the very brink of bankruptcy. However, the challenge is not only, indeed not primarily, financial and material. It is above all political and conceptual: it lies in the policies and relations between different actors and in the mechanisms of response and assistance. Even in normal circumstances, the integration of different policies and forms of assistance into a coherent, unified approach and the effective co-ordination of the actors associated with foreign assistance, with the optimal alignment of external support with local efforts, have proved difficult in the context of development co-operation. They have proved even more difficult where they are most important – in regard to emergency assistance in conflict situations.

In the view of the designers of a major on-going research project on 'Problems of International Assistance in Post-Conflict Situations':

> it is the present incapacity of the international community to live up to this challenge that explains the apparent preponderance of failures over successes [in the search for peace and the return to sustainable development] and that leads to a general uneasiness about current operations and forms of international response.[3]

A critical lack of clarity exists in at least three fundamental policy areas, it is suggested:

• confusion exists as to the relative policy mix with which the international community should intervene in post-conflict situations; in essence, how to integrate into one coherent approach different tools and forms of action – humanitarian, developmental, political and military – so that they reinforce each other, rather than operate independently or against each other;

• confusion at the institutional and the operational level; this is

particularly true with respect to the relative responsibilities and
mandates of the different actors involved in international assistance and
co-operation, different departments and agencies of the UN and other
multilateral bodies, bilateral actors and the non-governmental
organization (NGO) community;

• confusion and much political ambiguity characterize the relations
between 'external' and 'local' actors in conflicts; that is, between the
international community and what remains of state and local authorities,
local NGOs and civil society.[4]

The Essential Agenda

To meet the challenge of sustaining societal values and capacities through
conflicts and rebuilding conflict-stricken communities, requires the pursuit,
in an integrated, comprehensive and sensitive manner, of at least eight
related objectives:

• demilitarization, which includes demobilization, disarmament,
demining, reintegration of the military into civil society and the
economy;

• the continuation and then careful phasing-out of humanitarian and
emergency relief;

• political reconstruction, including support for the organization of
elections;

• social reconstruction and the rebuilding of human capacities to engage
in worthwhile economic, social, cultural and political activities, in a way
that permits both self-fulfilment and respect for the rights of others;

• economic reconstruction, including the identification of means of
entering the global economy, without the risk of renewed collapse and
conflict;

• rebuilding respect for basic human rights and establishing mechanisms
for their promotion and monitoring;

• support for the formulation of new shared visions – among communities
and nations – for it is the realization of such societal visions that the
author believes constitutes the best definition of development;

• capacity building, that unglamorous, essential responsibility of UNDP
within the UN system, which relates to all these objectives.

Designing a More Appropriate International Response System

This elaboration of some of the challenges of peace-building suggests certain principles upon which a concerted strategy and mechanisms might be constructed.

First, there is a need for all actors to remain responsive to the values, the needs, the justified aspirations and the initiatives of affected societies and communities.

Secondly, it is important to emphasize at all stages of UN operations the recognition, the utilization and the strengthening of local coping capacities, including the capacity to assume responsibility for the new challenges of reconstruction and development.

Thirdly, the value of joint analysis between local actors and the international community of underlying causes of conflict in terms of peace-building and the potential for renewed social harmony and sustainable development needs to be emphasized. Such an approach should help to bring the insights and the strengths of both parties to bear on the formulation of coherent conflict responses.

Fourthly, there is a need for collective recommendations, in terms of mandates and objectives, to be presented in a coherent framework to which all are committed.

Fifthly, the scope needs to be explored for integrated programmes which bring together the concerned actors under a single (and preferably shared) management structure to relate in a unified manner and to share new visions and collective action, which are such an important part of the healing process.

Sixthly, there is a need for the integration of the approaches adopted by the military arm of peace missions with the advice and proposals of political and human rights specialists and development managers. It is unlikely that any one of these mission elements has the full range of relevant information nor the diverse capacities and methodologies required to respond adequately to complex and socially sensitive situations.

Seventhly, the importance needs to be stressed of ensuring that such integration is respected globally, regionally, nationally and locally; and that there are specific mechanisms for group recommendations to emerge from each level and be shared effectively with all relevant bodies.

Eighthly, there is a need for each mission element to be so organized that it can speak with a unified and equal voice in the search for integrated approaches. This is especially important for the humanitarian and development components where there is less experience in developing common positions.

Ninthly, the importance of mutual respect and commitment to draw on comparative strengths and recognize the comparative responsibilities of each mission entity should be stressed.

Tenthly, the absolute imperative should be stressed of sustained and predictable funding if integrated approaches are to be adopted and are to make a useful contribution to long-term solutions to complex emergencies. This calls for active and sustained resource-mobilization strategies in which all parties are involved. This includes national or local leaders, peacekeeping officers, political and human rights advisers and humanitarian and development specialists.

Lastly, there is a need for flexible funding. The method of providing support is likely to be as important to the outcome as the scale of it. This means that special emphasis must be placed on the design of flexible mechanisms that allow resources to be transferred to meet emerging opportunities, which may range from peacekeeping, to humanitarian relief, to development and to human rights initiatives.

In short, the imperatives of the situation call for: greater co-ordination; clear comprehensive strategies; integrated action; flexible management partnerships; and sustained and flexible funding.

Taking Stock of Current Performance

In reviewing material on recent UN combined peacekeeping, humanitarian relief and reconstruction operations it is interesting to examine the excellent 'Comprehensive Report on Lessons Learned from United Nations Operation in Somalia'.[5] The author was an observer of the Somalia operations from neighbouring Kenya from 1992 to 1995, where he was responsible for co-ordination of the cross-border operations that led to the successful repatriation of over a quarter of a million refugees from north-eastern Kenya to areas of Somalia that were – except for a brief and bloody interlude in early 1992 – beyond the reach both of the warring factions and of the UN Operation in Somalia (UNOSOM). This report states that:

> The United Nations must pursue an integrated strategy aimed at supporting the judiciary, police, local government, the economy, reconciliation, disarmament, and demobilization.[6]

Having read such an unequivocal statement of commitment to the integration of development into complex peace operations, the author searched in vain for any reference to modalities that would ensure the effective participation of development specialists and development co-operation managers in the process. In fact, it shows that from the very design of the report, as in the formulation of the UNOSOM operations themselves, the development community had been left out.

The four syndicates established to review the operation covered: Security Council mandates; political and associated institution building; humanitarian aspects and information management; and military aspects. Time and again in the report, one reads that it is essential to have an integrated mission plan covering political, humanitarian and military aspects, without even a mention of development. In short, in theory as in practice it appears that despite the recognition that peace and development are intertwined, when it comes to emergency operations, development is put on hold.

The cynical observer might suggest that for high-risk operations that all too often fail to achieve their objectives and end in confusion and ignominious retreat from bold beginnings, this has at least the advantage of safeguarding the credibility of development. This may, in fact, be an asset when development organizations are, as often happens, left to pick up the pieces and carry on after the withdrawal of the peacekeepers.

Integrating Development into Peace Operations

It is well known that the UN system was conceived as a federal structure, with few effective mechanisms for achieving synergy and concerted action. This has had some notable advantages in terms of the mobilization of communities, interest groups, constituencies and resources in support of the specific goals of organizations within the UN, but it has not favoured a co-ordinated response to complex challenges.

Even within the UN Secretariat through the 1970s and the 1980s, there was a sharp divide between the operations of the Peacekeeping and the Political Department, on the one hand, and the funds and programmes responsible for Humanitarian Assistance and Development on the other. The fact that for development, operational responsibility was shared with a wide range of more than 20 autonomous, specialized agencies, each with its own mandate, its own constituency and its own governance has compounded the problem. It has also been impossible to engage the best-resourced institutions of the UN system – the Bretton Woods institutions – with their different stake holders, at a global or country level.

In the 1990s attempts have been made to introduce a minimum of order and concerted conduct among the organizations engaged in humanitarian assistance. The Department of Humanitarian Affairs (DHA) was established in 1992 to act, with technical and operational support from an Inter Agency Standing Committee, as a focal point for the consolidation of UN efforts in this area. Yet the mandate and the authority of the DHA remain ambiguous, its resources, capacity and operational experience far too limited to allow it to live up to the immensity of its tasks.

As for development, the painfully slow progress towards more integrated strategies appeared to have been reversed when, in 1993, the Office of the Director General for Development and International Economic Co-operation – that think-tank of just a dozen officials with the unenviable task of ensuring coherence among the activities of the UN system in all its non-political work – was dissolved. This left a critical gap. However, it was only in 1995 that the UN Secretary-General entrusted a single official – the Administrator of UNDP – with responsibility for assisting him in the substantive co-ordination of the work of the several funds and programmes engaged in operational activities operating under the general authority of the General Assembly. The thinking behind this was to encourage the autonomous specialized agencies to collaborate around agreed goals and to mobilize for these same purposes the support of the Bretton Woods institutions.

Given such a general lack of fully-legitimized and accepted co-ordinating structures working in humanitarianism, it is not surprising that it has been difficult for the many involved partners to voice their concerns effectively.

With respect to the broader challenge of designing and implementing peace operations, in 1993, following the realization that new-style peacekeeping missions increasingly had the objective of saving the lives of millions of civilians trapped in conflicts, weekly meetings were established between the Under-Secretary-Generals (USGs) for Peacekeeping, Political Affairs and Humanitarian Affairs. Yet here again, it was only in 1995 that the Administrator of UNDP was added to the group to ensure that underlying developmental concerns would also be addressed.

Clearly something more is needed if the UN is to be empowered and equipped to rise to the challenge of integrated operations and I would suggest that the following might be explored:

• the full involvement of UN development specialists in early warning systems;

• that comprehensive assessments of emerging situations, under the direct authority of the Secretary-General, should be undertaken, drawing on all relevant information. Development co-operation managers, as in early warning systems, would have an important role and should be associated with the preparation and the presentation of analyses;

• the design of preventive development strategies, as an essential complement to preventive diplomacy and preventive humanitarian actions should be undertaken;

• the development and presentation to the SC of truly comprehensive peace strategies should be undertaken, that build on the analysis of underlying causes and suggest how these might be addressed; this would involve not only the country or local populations concerned but also regional structures and the UN; these strategies should be updated regularly so that linkages and shifts of emphasis over time may be developed against an agreed common framework.

In theory, the co-ordination of UN activities at country level is clear. First, under normal circumstances, team leadership is assumed by a single official – the Resident Co-ordinator of the Operational Activities for Development. In reality, the mandate of the Resident Co-ordinator took three years to negotiate and when it emerged from a gruelling process of inter-agency compromise it was couched more in terms of 'thou shalt not', rather than in terms of what could be done. Naturally, no specific resources accompanied it, and it was only in 1989 that the role of the Resident Co-ordinator in emergency situations was finally recognized.

Nevertheless, it is the task of these Co-ordinators, who are drawn from an increasingly wide range of UN bodies and serve as the Resident Representatives of UNDP, to ensure that the focus of country work remains on development. Where the role of Resident Co-ordinator is exercised with appropriate initiative and imagination and in a spirit of partnership and facilitation with the other members of a country group of team-leaders, the Resident Co-ordinator system has served as a useful countervailing force to the pressures for fragmentation that come both from within the UN system and generally from the host country. The mandate of the Resident Co-ordinator has recently been clarified in an attempt to prepare the UN system for more coherent and integrated approaches to the development challenges recently identified by the international community. New approaches, including the establishment of task-teams on specific issues, have been adopted, and, for the first time, a modicum of resources has been made available – by UNDP.

Similarly, in the case of natural and limited man-made disasters, the Resident Co-ordinator is now responsible for establishing and leading the UN Disaster Management Team and promoting multi-disciplinary and developmentally sound approaches to emergency situations.

For complex operations involving peacekeeping, the situation is different. Most frequently the Secretary-General designates a Special Representative with full responsibility for negotiating and implementing the peace process, managing the input of the UN Secretariat, mobilizing the support of the operational funds and programmes for humanitarian and development activities and leading the team of autonomous specialized agencies. The transfer of important responsibilities from the Resident Co-ordinator to the Special Representative of the Secretary-General (SRSG) and from the SRSG back to a Co-ordinator has proved problematic.

One solution that is currently being explored is the designation of the Resident Co-ordinator (serving both as Humanitarian and Development Co-ordinator) as Deputy to the SRSG. This should help to redress the imbalance between the military/political aspects of operations and those relating more directly to the immediate needs and the longer-term goals of the civil population. Among the mechanisms at the disposal of the SRSG and the Resident Co-ordinator to ensure the integration of development concerns are: the Country Strategy Note; the recently introduced Common Country Assessment; and consolidated appeals. In reality, despite the clear mandate of the SRSG, the existence of the Resident Co-ordinator system and the introduction of the mechanisms described earlier, the achievement of unity among the components of peace operations, along with the integration of development concerns into peace missions, is fraught with difficulty.

From personal observation and experience and on the lessons learned from the analysis of recent UN peace missions, the following thoughts may be useful in achieving more effective co-ordination on the ground:

- The SRSG needs to be not only an experienced negotiator with political skills, but also an effective manager of a complex organization and excellent mobilizer of public support and resources.

- There is a need for clear structures for regular co-ordination among all key partners; these may include the holding of daily briefing sessions among all senior staff, including the humanitarian and development Co-ordinator, and regular sessions with a broader grouping of all humanitarian and developmental agencies.

- It is essential to develop clear, comprehensive operational strategies – if necessary for different parts of a country or region – against which resources may be mobilized and assigned, initiatives taken and security underwritten; on the few occasions where this has been achieved the results appear to be highly successful.

- In the new South Africa great emphasis is justifiably placed on the development of group dynamics and team work, especially at the executive and managerial levels of government and business; this seems an ideal approach to the development of a unified team of team leaders and decision makers around an SRSG.

- Given the need for military and civilian staff to share or exchange responsibilities regularly, it is essential that there should be standardized training for functions across the military/civilian divide which should draw on the best practices of each element; this would, however, certainly require give and take on both sides.

- Respect for the principle of transparency – within the confines of collective confidentiality – among the key actors under the responsibility of the SRSG is indispensable. It is essential that the non-military mission elements are aware of the intentions of the military and that the military be kept fully abreast of initiatives to be undertaken under humanitarian and developmental programmes: this was demonstrated by the incident in Mogadishu in which the entire senior management team of UNDP was held hostage at gun point overnight by US forces operating under the aegis of UNOSOM II.

- Given the intense degree of interest in peace operations by local populations and international media alike, it is essential that the public information aspects of operations be formulated by the integrated team and that these should be the sole basis for the handling of public information by all the participating entities of the UN; the alternative is confusion, the provision of ample material for criticism and, in extreme cases, increased risk for the members of the UN programmes.

Establishing Partnerships with Local Communities

One of the greatest failures of the international community in conflict resolution has been the inability to relate effectively to those most seriously affected by conflict and crises; that is the local communities themselves. Faced with the need to save lives, humanitarian assistance managers and to a greater extent peacekeepers are unlikely to realize that their well-intentioned actions could endanger the very livelihoods of those they are striving to help.

There is an urgent need to adopt a completely new approach, in which the intended beneficiaries of peace operations are fully associated with the search for solutions. This does not mean the multiplication of interminable and often divisive high-level conferences – although these certainly have their place when conditions are right – but rather the development, despite the difficulties involved, of discreet, sensitive contacts. This may be achieved through informal channels and with local groups of all kinds, when the capacity to listen and to observe and thus to gain insights is developed. An understanding of local aspirations and processes must be the basis of sustainable solutions.

An example of the failure to recognize and build upon the under-estimated strengths and resources of communities, especially in Africa, has been the neglect of the women's peace movements. In recent years, women's groups across the African continent have struggled to make an impact on the peace processes. They have lacked resources, formal structures and frequently have been without a voice in the design of relief and rehabilitation operations that have tended to be both necessitated and dominated by men. A programme that has tried to do something about this and has achieved a great deal in a short time in Sudan, Somalia, Rwanda and Burundi and elsewhere, through the empowering of women to express their views and to make a direct contribution to the improvement of their own situation, is the African Women in Crisis Programme (AFWIC), sponsored by the UN Fund for Women (UNIFEM). It helped to make the contribution of women to the search for peace one of the high-points of the fourth International Conference on Women in Beijing in 1995. Yet this initiative still goes unnoticed in many UN and regional circles, suffers from totally inadequate core support and is dependent for its effectiveness on the often fleeting interest of individual donors. When one talks of local actors, one often forgets the female half of the population which is left to cope with the responsibilities and the suffering that the other half has usually imposed upon it.

It has been noted that:

> an integral part of any United Nations peacekeeping missions should be the promotion of 'indirect peace-building'.[7]

In other words, support for the revival of associational life and the resurrection of a web of civic, professional, business, athletic and other associations is a major component of the reconciliation process in war-torn societies in terms of building multiple bridges across lines of conflict and improving lines of communication. Civil society is the backbone of a sustainable political system. Its resuscitation in a collapsed state is a long-term process and ultimately the responsibility of the people themselves. Nevertheless, the international community has a potentially constructive role to play in catalysing these developments.

In peace operations, an essential component must be the design and creation of a safe political space, so that elements of civil society may re-emerge without fear of intimidation and retaliation. Within the UN the closest linkages with the local populations are likely to be found among those elements who have been the development partners of a society. They generally constitute an under-utilized source of advice, ideas, knowledge, experience and commitment that could surely benefit peace operations as a whole. The local developmental NGO community is normally even better qualified to play an advisory role, although it is just as likely as others to be diverted from its long-term objectives by pressing humanitarian imperatives.

Financing of Development Activities within UN Peace Missions

A major obstacle to successful peace operations in recent times has been the lack of financial resources commensurate with the mandates assigned by the international community to the UN. When the multiplicity of mission components – political, humanitarian and developmental – that are the key to the sustainability of peace initiatives are added the challenge is even greater.

Although it is essential to be cautious in making financial demands and to take account of current constraints on national budgets in all parts of the world, being realistic in predicting the impact of under-funded or incomplete operations is equally important. It may even lead to the recognition that the net effect of operations that cannot be sustained could be negative. Successful peacekeeping is costly, especially when operations are conceived as global rather than as regional exercises. However, the total impact of the massive investments involved in peacekeeping may be greatly enhanced and the long-term costs reduced if the military intervention is accompanied by the other measures that are needed to achieve lasting solutions and to tackle underlying causes. Yet it is exactly these that are normally left to voluntary contributions and are thus the first to feel the impact of budgetary cut-backs. A number of measures that should accompany military peace operations have been referred to here: the need for political initiatives; community involvement; for public information that engages the local population; politically constructive humanitarian initiatives; the reconstruction of basic infrastructure; support for the rebuilding of civil society; and the retraining of demobilized military personnel. These and other measures, should be given active consideration. Few of the societies that have collapsed in the aftermath of the Cold War have the means to return rapidly and safely to normality and to the kind of sustainable development that enables each member of society to survive and flourish. This is not surprising. It took a massive injection of external support, provided with great generosity and without external conditionalities, to enable Western Europe to rise from the destruction of the Second World War. The starting point for most regions and countries emerging from conflict today is decidedly more challenging. What is needed is a steady, adequate and assured flow of international support, both for transitional humanitarian relief and for capacity-building development initiatives.

The scale and the impact on development of the new humanitarian demand may be demonstrated by the transformation of two of the UN's organizations from essentially developmental to largely emergency functions. A few years ago the World Food Programme (WFP) could devote some 65 per cent of its resources to development and 35 per cent to humanitarian food relief. Today the proportions have been reversed. Meanwhile, for non-food items the UN International Children's Emergency Fund (UNICEF) has seen its emergency contributions grow to a level that equals its development resources, while the latter have stagnated at constant levels in US dollar terms. Overseas development administration flows are under attack everywhere.

Despite the difficulties in recent years of ensuring adequate replenishment of the concessionary loan funds of the World Bank, the negotiated obligatory contributions to the international financial institutions represent a major element in the total funding available for development. However, these resources are not normally available to countries whose basic institutions of financial management and organized banking have collapsed.

Conclusions and Recommendations

This analysis suggests that the international community should consider a number of options and initiatives. First, it is essential to examine the cost effectiveness of the several forms of intervention. This will entail looking at new partnerships. This might include a partnership in which regional military contingents – in Africa mobilized jointly through the OAU and relevant sub-regional institutions – would be fully financed at regionally-determined rates by the international community through the UN and under the general authority of the SC.

Secondly, comprehensive cost estimates for peace operations should be presented to the SC and, afterwards, to the international community as a whole. These should include specific provisions, based on the ground assessments by multi-disciplinary teams, of aspects that must be addressed to give the mission a reasonable chance of success. What is essential is that there should be an opportunity to review the peace initiatives as a whole and that international commitment is written into the process, rather than the stop-gap measures designed to avert immediate catastrophes or respond to sudden disasters that have tended to prevail.

Thirdly, the organization of a series of resource mobilization initiatives is required. These could involve the presentation of a broad-based peace operation plan to a special international conference. The proposals would probably be area-specific and would again be based on ground assessments.

Fourthly, far greater flexibility in implementation is required. We, in the development field, have the advantage of being used to a great deal of delegated authority and the associated procedures for ensuring full accountability. This spirit needs to pervade other aspects of UN peace missions. Flexibility is also required in the grey areas of responsibility. The managers of military and political processes, for example, need to be able to deploy supplementary humanitarian or basic physical development resources in support of their initiatives. Development co-operation specialists should be associated with these types of operation to ensure sustainability and community involvement. There also needs to be a mechanism to allow the transfer of humanitarian resources to development, whenever the situation allows this.

Fifthly, new partnerships must be forged between the regions and institutions that still have substantial resources for development co-operation – the European Union, the World Bank, Japan and the newly industrialized countries of south-east Asia – and those who are best placed to undertake development co-operation on the ground in times of crisis. At the national level, the UN development system is normally best placed to engage in capacity-building and institutional strengthening, including support for the re-emergence of viable and legitimate state structures that must provide the basic framework for law and order, justice, basic human services and the planning and maintenance of essential infrastructure. UN organizations, together with the NGO community (local and international), community-based organizations and above all the communities themselves, should be engaged in the implementation of grass-roots initiatives that are the key to the restoration of health and dynamism in society at large. New partnerships should also be explored with the private sector. The example of South Africa has shown the potentially positive impact on peaceful political transition of a responsible private sector with an eye for its own long-term interests. There must be scope for harnessing far more effectively the imagination and the resources of the private sector, international and local, formal and informal, in the search for renewed development and economic growth.

Finally, and this point cannot be made strongly enough, there is a need for sustained international financial support in terms of positive resource flows to countries and regions in crisis. As a first step, the debt overhang, which combined with structural adjustment packages has brought nations across Africa to their knees, must be tackled. There must also be adequate financial support to safeguard the livelihoods of the most vulnerable, including whole communities and small nations, as they struggle to adapt to the competition of the global marketplace. And there must be strong commitment to providing the means that will allow nations either to recover past economic strength or to break out, possibly for the first time, from the vicious circle of poverty and under-capacity.

In March 1996, the Secretary-General launched the *UN System-wide Special Initiative on Africa*. The proposals advanced build on Africa's own priorities as set out most recently in the Cairo Declaration of the Heads of

State of the OAU. They call for additional effort on the part of Africa's partners in addressing debt overhang and funding essential human development activities. Yet, in so doing, they merely reiterate the need for the international community to respect the commitments entered into in the 1980s in a compact designed to underpin the radical, courageous and often destabilizing reforms adopted by Africa. It requires the international community's continued moral, technical and above all financial support for the implementation of these commitments.

The response to the call by the Secretary-General, by the Administrator of UNDP and the Executive Secretary of the United Nations Economic Commission for Africa, with formal endorsement by the President of Ethiopia on behalf of the OAU, will determine to a great extent whether the international community is ready and the UN equipped to play their roles as development partners of countries in crisis in Africa.

NOTES

The opinions expressed in this article are exclusively those of the author and do not represent the views of the UN or the UNDP.

1. James Gustave Speth, 'Why the United Nations is Essential to Successful Development Co-operation (and vice versa)', New York: UNDP, 17 Jan. 1996, p.4.
2. Ibid., p.5.
3. 'Rebuilding War-torn Societies: an Action-Research Project on Problems of International Assistance in Post-Conflict Situations', Geneva: UN Research Institute for Social Development and the Programme for Strategic and International Studies, Geneva Graduate Institute of International Studies, Mar. 1995, pp.1–3.
4. Ibid., p.2.
5. 'Comprehensive Report on Lessons Learned from United Nations Operations in Somalia, April 1992 – March 1995', Friedrich Ebert Stiftung, Life and Peace Institute of Sweden, and the Norwegian Institute of International Affairs, in co-operation with the Lessons Learned Unit of the UN Department of Peacekeeping Operations, Dec. 1995, pp.1–24.
6. Ibid., p.12.
7. Ibid.

The Stretcher and the Drum: Civil-Military Relations in Peace Support Operations

HUGO SLIM

This article examines the relationship between international military forces and civilian humanitarian organizations, and looks at how these two groups perceive one another. First, it compares military and humanitarian organizational cultures. Secondly, it considers the terms 'military' and 'humanitarian' to show how each encompasses a range of differing organizational cultures, making operational planning and standardized practice more complicated than is commonly recognized. Thirdly, having identified two main types of civil-military relationship in peace-support operations – technical and security relationships – it identifies several areas of tension and consensus between the two groups. The article ends by outlining policy and practice conclusions for those responsible for managing civil-military co-operation in emergencies.

Although relationships between civilian humanitarians and the military have increased and intensified in recent years, they are by no means new. Modern humanitarianism was founded on the battlefield, and inevitably there has always been contact between military forces and humanitarian organizations, albeit to a varying degree. In the nineteenth century the International Committee of the Red Cross (ICRC), the world's first modern international, humanitarian organization, was founded after the Battle of Solferino. In the twentieth century, war in Europe and elsewhere also produced a number of outstanding individual humanitarians, and a range of humanitarian organizations.[1] The First World War, and the civil war and famine which followed it in Russia, galvanized Eglantyne Jebb and others to establish the Save the Children Fund, with its declaration of child rights. Both conflicts also saw the first operations of the American Relief Association under Herbert Hoover. Similarly, humanitarian agencies – such as Oxfam and CARE – emerged out of the Second World War. Thus to a large degree modern humanitarianism may be said to have been born out of war.

This article focuses on the relationship between international military

Hugo Slim is Director of the Centre for Development and Emergency Planning at Oxford Brookes University.

forces and civilian humanitarian organizations. Its purpose is to look at how these two groups perceive one another; it does not examine the operational mechanisms they use to co-operate and liaise at field level. It is essentially concerned with international military forces and international humanitarian organizations, and consequently does not specifically explore international military relations with national non-governmental organizations (NGOs) nor with civilian commercial companies. While it is vital that such relations should be better understood, such a task lies beyond the scope of this article.

The Stretcher and the Drum

Walking in their wake, humanitarianism is all too familiar with the activities of armies and their consequences. Like liquor sellers and prostitutes, humanitarians could also be described as camp followers, because with their stretchers and their aid they too follow the drum. For the last 100 years, militarism and humanitarianism have represented two sides of the same coin – humankind's inability to manage conflict peacefully. In many ways military and humanitarian organizations find themselves as much connected as separated by their common roots in war. By a strange paradox, a nobility is attached to both militarism and humanitarianism. There is a perceived nobility in killing and in dying, and there is a nobility too in saving life. In many societies both activities are looked upon as heroic. In support of this idea a number of people combine both professions in a single life, with the traffic being mostly one way, from soldier to humanitarian. Such links between the two professions do seem to indicate that militarism and humanitarianism share certain values such as service, courage, endurance, selflessness, organizational loyalty, adventure and prestige.[2]

A Peculiar Mimicry

Through this strange mimicry, which extends into their organizational cultures and behaviour, both military and humanitarian organizations use similar language: they work 'in the field', where it is often 'officers' who manage 'operations', while frequently reporting to 'headquarters'. From an anthropologist's perspective, Benthall has observed how NGOs, with their logos and flags have a form of 'heraldic coat of arms'.[3] But sometimes such mimicry is not purely symbolic. A vignette from relief operations during the Italian invasion of Ethiopia in 1936 is instructive:

> I kept the convoy close together and placed guards on the roof of the lorries. I squatted on top of the leading lorry myself with my Winchester between my knees.[4]

To those of us schooled in post-war humanitarian neutrality, it is hard to believe that this is a description of the ICRC delegate to Ethiopia. But one need not look so far back as 1936 to see humanitarian agencies mimicking the military. The increasing use of private armed guards by civilian relief agencies in Iraq and Somalia since 1991 shows that we have almost come full circle. It also demonstrates that NGOs, in particular, are quite capable of militarizing their operations by themselves. They are so flexible, that when they have to they can even manage private armies. Such mirror-imaging works both ways and has been particularly extravagant in recent British Army advertising campaigns. These often show images of soldiers engaged in humanitarian work in an apparent effort to persuade would-be recruits to join up because joining the Army is really like joining an NGO.[5]

Despite this strange mutual emulation, it would be a gross simplification to conclude that the military and civilian humanitarians have everything in common and that they are somehow supremely compatible. This is not the case and should not be assumed by policy makers; they are also quite different. Despite apparently similar organizational behaviour, international humanitarian organizations tend to be made up of people who have profound reservations about militarism. 'Khaki' makes many of them extremely uneasy. Indeed, the reds, blues and whites of their own organizational plumage have deliberately evolved to set themselves strikingly apart from the colours of the military.

Gender is also a factor which accounts in part for inherent cultural differences between soldiers and humanitarians. While most military forces are still predominantly male, humanitarian organizations have a high proportion of female staff, increasingly in senior positions. It would be too simple to suggest that women do not subscribe to the macho culture of humanitarianism, but the high presence of women in humanitarian organizations does introduce a challenging gender factor into civil-military relations which may not exist to such a degree in military-military relations.

While the majority of soldiers have always found it easy and morally right to be humanitarian on occasion, the inverse is not the case. The majority of humanitarians do not find it easy, or morally right, to be militaristic and to use violence. Here, perhaps, is the rub in their relationship. One party disagrees fundamentally with the position of the other. At a profound moral level the humanitarian has more problems with the military than the military has with the humanitarian. The result is a reticence and ambivalence on the part of the humanitarian which extends beyond questions of operational procedure to matters of ethics and identity.

'Unpacking' both Parties

Before venturing more specifically into the nature of the relationship and the respective roles of the military and the humanitarian agencies in today's political emergencies and conflicts, it is important to identify more accurately the several parties in this relationship and what distinguishes their recent contact. In doing so it is essential to avoid the temptation to generalize, stereotype and caricature.

The 'Military'

Connaughton has rightly observed that the military are not monolithic and that use of the word 'military' must be treated with caution for two reasons.[6] First, because a military force may take many different forms; force size, structure, capability and posture may vary enormously. There is a big difference between a few UN guards armed with pistols and wearing baseball caps in Iraq and the massive power of the Unified Task Force (UNITAF) in Somalia or the Implementation Force (IFOR) in Bosnia. How a force is configured will affect what it can do, how it behaves, the impression it gives and the relationship people have with it.

Connaughton's second point is equally important. He notes that national militaries differ and that there are disparities in military competence and professionalism. In short, some nations are better than others. He has also made the point that some nation's forces are particularly good at some things and particularly bad at others, and therefore talks of there being 'forces for courses'.[7] There are currently more than 40 countries contributing troops to UN forces, and UN multinational military forces are usually made up of several different national forces. In such cases the recognition of differences within the force is vital.

Civilian Humanitarians

If the military are not monolithic neither are the civilian agencies. There are three main groupings of operational agencies which make up the international civilian humanitarian sector: UN agencies; the ICRC and the wider Red Cross movement; and NGOs (international and national). Each of the three organizational groupings is unique in character and mandate; a fact which inevitably affects its role and relationship with international military forces.

UN Agencies and the ICRC

Both the UN agencies and the ICRC are properly described as intergovernmental organizations (IGOs) because they are mandated by agreements drawn up between states: the UN Charter and conventions in the case of the UN agencies; the Geneva Conventions (1949) and their additional protocols (1977) in the case of the ICRC. The many articles in these international legal instruments give UN agencies and the ICRC specific mandates and operating procedures. Their clear international mandates make any military relations with these organizations more prescribed, ensuring that operational relationships are at least clear-cut, albeit not necessarily easy.

Central to the humanitarian response of the UN agencies is the role of 'the big four': the United Nations High Commissioner for Refugees (UNHCR); the World Food Programme (WFP); the United Nations Children's Fund (UNICEF); and the United Nations Development Programme (UNDP).[8] In most emergencies these agencies are more operational than other UN bodies. But UNDP's frequent failure to play an effective lead role in emergencies has meant that the United Nations Department of Humanitarian Affairs (UNDHA), which was created in 1992, now ranks as a main player, although its role is one of co-ordination and its influence and impact vary greatly from one emergency to another. The operational presence and individual mandates of the big four and UNDHA make them the most likely UN agencies to come into close contact with international military forces.

International NGOs

Diversity and proliferation are bywords for describing today's NGO sector. Describing the difference between the two major operational components of civilian humanitarian agencies, Donini has compared the 'rapidly evolving NGO galaxy' to the 'not-so-rapidly evolving UN solar system'. There is no doubt that there are many more national and international NGOs in existence than there were ten years ago, and that these are taking a much greater share of humanitarian assistance budgets than before. Reports of there being some 175 international NGOs in Kigali in 1994, 100 in Goma, 200 operating out of Zagreb, and 200 in Mozambique are frequently repeated. But despite the prevailing image of rampant NGO proliferation which such figures create, there are two reasons why the apparent confusion on the ground is perhaps less significant than these figures might lead us to believe.

First, the high profile emergencies (such as Rwanda and Bosnia) tend to skew the global facts somewhat, because many of what the UN Secretary-General has called the 'orphan emergencies' (such as Angola, Liberia and Sierra Leone) have involved NGOs numbered in tens rather than hundreds.[9] Secondly, and perhaps more importantly, a high proportion of funding in any emergency (high profile or not) actually goes to a relatively small number of big international NGOs. Donini uses the language of the mafia when referring to the view of one senior UN official that there is now an:

> oligopoly where eight major families or federations of international NGOs have come to control almost half of an $8 billion market.[10]

Natsios notes rightly that most NGOs are not involved in relief. He makes the point that there are:

> perhaps 20 in the US and another 20 in Europe that work in complex emergencies [whose] work is sustained, technically sound and widespread enough to have an impact on the ground.[11]

Of these 40 NGOs he estimates that perhaps ten US and another ten European NGOs receive 75 per cent of all the public funds spent by NGOs in complex emergencies. Ten US NGOs received 76 per cent of all cash grants to NGOs for relief purposes from the US government and over 87 per cent of all food aid for relief purposes in 1993. The European Union (EU) gave 65 per cent of all relief grants to 20 NGOs in 1994.[12]

It seems possible to conclude from this that, although NGO proliferation is a distinctive feature of today's emergencies, a more significant fact perhaps is that there is a definite premier league of international NGOs which in reality dominate humanitarian operations.[13] When discussing military-civil relations it is, therefore, important to distinguish between military relations with big and with small NGOs. Among the latter must be included the majority of national NGOs.

No summary of the NGO sector would be complete without reference to their notorious independence. In contrast with UN agencies and the Red Cross movement, NGOs determine their own mission and mandate. They write their own charters and prescribe their own values and principles.[14] This gives them a freedom which they are determined to maintain and means that any consensus across the NGO sector about a mission and mandate will often be variable and cast in the broadest terms. It can seldom be assumed that every NGO will be singing the same song in a given situation. Such independence has important consequences for the civil-military relationship and may make NGOs unpredictable and even tempestuous partners. Finally, as with the military so with NGOs – some are better than others and uneven quality, particularly among smaller NGOs, is as much a feature of the international NGO sector as it is of the international military sector.

Overlapping Roles

To appreciate the dynamics of the civil-military relationship in today's emergencies requires an understanding of the roles of the several parties concerned. This reveals where military and civilian operations overlap, and in what situations relationships, good or bad, develop. What is distinctive about the contact they have made in recent years?

Policy Relations

At a policy level the recent coalescence of international security policy with humanitarian concerns may at last have thrown together two natural partners, who had long been intended for one another but who had never actually met during the Cold War. Many commentators have noted how Cold War *realpolitik* ensured that international military force was never allowed to be considered as an option in responding to humanitarian crises. Donini puts it well when he describes the unnatural 'separateness' that grew up between international humanitarian and security policy in the Cold War. He notes how this resulted in:

> a separate development of the clusters of UN activity dealing with political and peacekeeping affairs from those dealing with human rights and humanitarian activities.[15]

In contrast, the relative consensus between the Permanent Five (P5) members of the UN Security Council (SC) after the Cold War has given that body supreme authority in shaping humanitarian policy and put it firmly into the driving seat of humanitarian affairs.[16]

At the policy level new contacts have been made between the international security community and humanitarians. The UN Secretariat now has a greatly improved military planning and command capacity. SC members are now frequently engaged by policy makers and lobbyists from humanitarian organizations. Military leaders from a number of countries have been propelled into the hot seat of humanitarian politics, while NGOs and academics working on disarmament, global security and conflict resolution have also suddenly become engaged in humanitarian affairs.

Operational Relations

The consequences of this newly merged security/humanitarian policy environment are felt most obviously by humanitarian and military practitioners at field level. It is here, above all, that the military and the civilian humanitarians meet, in a setting unfamiliar at least to the post-Second World War generation of soldiers and humanitarians. The new operational roles mandated to outside military forces, usually by Security Council Resolutions (SCRs), are described by general terms such as: military humanitarianism; 'wider' peacekeeping; or peace-support operations. These may broadly be divided into the three tasks of relief assistance, protection and peace-building.

On occasion, the military operate like a relief agency and become involved direct in the emergency provision of water, medical care and logistics support – Goma being the obvious example. On other occasions the military's mandate is concerned more with the protection of populations or of relief agencies and supplies, and with the consequent forceful containment and/or resolution of conflict – for example, Bosnia and Somalia. At other times the military are required to engage in peace-building within a peace process by disarming, demobilizing and reconstituting armed forces and overseeing elections: Cambodia, Mozambique and IFOR being examples. The kinds of civil-military relationship which develop on the ground are inevitably determined in part by which mode the military are operating in; whether it is provision, protection, peace-building, or a combination of all three. But in general, civil-military interactions may be characterized as technical or security relationships.

In a technical relationship there is obviously an element of overlap. Such overlap might be greatest when, as relief providers, military forces are working in precisely the same fields as civilian humanitarian NGOs, as in the provision of water, health, infrastructure and transport. In such situations, the civil-military relationship is primarily a technical and logistical one.

In a security relationship, military forces might be protecting civilian relief agencies or populations being served by civilian agencies. While in a peace-building mode military forces may develop technical and/or security relationships. Military operations concerned with de-mining, demobilization, election monitoring and the implementation of peace agreements all overlap with civilian humanitarian operations, which are similarly engaged with the same populations and processes.

Areas of Tension and Consensus

Much of the debate to date about civil-military relations in humanitarian operations has tended to focus on the differences. While these obviously exist between the two groups, there are also views, approaches, operational challenges and dilemmas which they have in common. In discussing the relationship it is therefore important not to make it into a bigger problem than it is, but also to consider the areas of agreement and opportunity.

A Shared Analysis

After five years of working in the same emergencies, military and civilian agencies do agree on some fundamental issues of humanitarian policy. Increasingly one hears both groups saying the same thing about two aspects of the humanitarian endeavours in which they are engaged.

First, both parties recognize the limits of humanitarianism; they emphasize that humanitarian assistance and military intervention are by no means solutions to political emergencies and conflict. Neither approach makes peace in itself. Leaders of the military, UN agencies, the ICRC and NGOs are all vocal on this point: that their interventions are no substitute for political settlements and subsequent development. Interestingly, statements made by the Director of Oxfam and a former Commander of the United Nations Protection Force in Former Yugoslavia (UNPROFOR) are almost interchangeable on this point.[17]

Secondly, having agreed upon this, both parties also seem to agree upon the fact that international aid policy is not consistently committed to the kinds of long-term political and developmental solution needed to achieve real peace. In their own operations both parties are increasingly aware of the constraints placed upon them by the political masters who dictate their mandates, the level of their resources and the policy environment in which they are required to work. Military commanders are only too well aware that:

> the military will only perform to the level of ability that their government will allow. Military professionalism cannot compensate for the absence of political will.[18]

Such a view is resonant of the bitter feelings of powerlessness experienced by UN forces in Bosnia and Rwanda. Similarly, civilian agencies talk about being donor-led and criticize the essentially 'aid-only' approach of Western governments to political emergencies. Such a policy, they claim, makes no serious efforts to address the root causes of conflict by investing in conflict prevention, and also stops short of long-term developmental, juridical and political initiatives in the aftermath of war. The impression gained from the statements of both military and civilian agencies is that both parties have a sense of being used, or even abused, to some degree by a prevailing Western policy framework which is at best selective and at worst actively disengaging from an investment in peace.

Security Relationships: The Consent Factor

From this it is logical to move to an assessment of overlapping operational relationships, starting with security-based relationships. Civil-military contact at field level is where the most intense relationships are formed. The nature of the civil-military security relationship is determined by the level of consent to military presence and action which exists in emergencies. By consent, military analysts mean the level of understanding, acceptance, popularity and support of the military force and its mission. As recent humanitarian operations have shown, consent in these situations refers not only to the primary consent of the local population but also to the additional consent of civilian humanitarian agencies. When levels of consent run low, civil-military relationships become strained and civilian humanitarians distance themselves from the military.

As the military manuals are quick to point out, consent is not a constant but a variable commodity. The level of consent with which a force arrives may not be that with which it leaves. Similarly, the level of consent for the same military force may differ from one geographical area to another. Consent may, therefore, vary over time and space. As a result consent in a peace-support military operation has to be continuously managed and nurtured.

To illustrate the link between consent and civil-military relations, Weiss has ranked all recent UN military humanitarian operations in order of consent level.[19] He has identified seven points along a spectrum of varying consent, with Cambodia, Mozambique and El Salvador at the high end and Bosnia and Somalia at the low end. His analysis confirms what all civilian humanitarian agencies have discovered to their cost: that the more closely associated a civilian agency is with an unpopular international military force, the less room for manoeuvre that agency has; and that civil-military relations become problematic in these circumstances.

Problems of Over-identification

Civilian humanitarian organizations find themselves in a real dilemma in their relationships with military forces where consent is low, in that the very alliance which often facilitates their humanitarian programmes may be the same association which undermines their position and credibility in the eyes of local groups. Paradoxically, the protection of civilian agencies may increase their vulnerability. This dilemma helps to explain the essential ambivalence in civilian organizations' attitude to, and relationship with, the military, which many commentators have described in terms of 'mixed feelings'. Their dilemma is well expressed in the final statement from a meeting of European NGOs in Brussels in 1994:

> In some cases, an international military presence has enabled NGOs to operate when they otherwise could not. Yet in others, as at times in Somalia, the level of violence caused partly by UN forces has made it difficult or impossible for NGOs to act. Military actions pose dangers which affect both the people with whom NGOs are working and NGOs' own programmes. In other situations, as at times in Bosnia-Herzegovina, NGOs' work has been threatened by the hostility of local civilians who perceive European NGOs as just part of an international community which had betrayed them by failing to use military force.[20]

Weiss sums up the trade-off involved:

> although military cover may be necessary and useful in some situations, the political cost to the neutral and impartial image of

humanitarians must be carefully weighed in each instance.[21]

As this implies, the military-civilian relationship must be constantly monitored and renegotiated as both parties keep a keen eye on the level of consent which pertains in terms of the military operation. Like many others, Oxfam has become well aware of the problem of humanitarian agencies becoming 'over-identified' with the military, and has suffered the consequences in terms of staff injuries, obstruction and the loss of popular or factional consent for its own programmes.[22]

The Need for Distancing

The dangers of too close an association with the military have often required civilian humanitarian organizations to distance themselves from military operations. On occasion such distancing has been suddenly and dramatically implemented in a flurry of press releases – baffling and even infuriating military personnel. Such doubletalk has given humanitarian organizations something of a reputation in military circles for equivocation.

Yet, if such talk has seemed ungracious, it has also been necessary. It is essential that military forces learn to discern the different audiences humanitarian pragmatists have to address in order to survive. Most civilian agencies have long-term commitments and investments in the countries in which they work. These require them to take the long view and to preserve their contacts, credibility and reputation, and to safeguard their staff and their infrastructure, which is vitally important to them. However, not all distancing will be tactical. In Somalia, for example, most of the civilian agencies were eventually genuinely appalled by the actions and policy of the US-led military forces. In this and other situations they spoke as much to the military themselves as to the 'gallery'.

An examination of the importance of consent as a factor in civil-military relations reveals that this valuable commodity is needed by civilian agencies as much as by the military. The loss of consent for military operations has something of a domino effect on civilian operations, which also need the consent of the local population and the local combatants to pursue their programmes. This seems to indicate that civilian and military organizations have a common problem in the maintenance of consent. Instead of being perceived simply as a tension in their relationship, the issue of consent should be regarded as an area where both parties should have an input in framing a joint policy. The generation, management and maintenance of consent is an obvious area for civil-military efforts to be combined.

Problems of Excessive Military Command

In many emergencies where the civil-military relationship has been primarily concerned with security and protection, the humanitarian organizations have felt hampered by the tendency of the political and military components of a UN peace operation to gain ascendancy over the humanitarian and developmental components. In Somalia UN and NGO agencies particularly felt increasingly marginalized as the chain of command and decision-making became predominantly political and military. For a peace operation to be effective in the long-term, the humanitarian and developmental aspects of the operation should be accorded equal value within any command structure, which should take the form of a triumvirate of the military, humanitarian and political elements. Most peace operations are not simply military operations, and the temptation for the military agenda to predominate must be resisted. This potential military bias in peace operations is noted by Save the Children UK:

> Without clear mandates and separate identities, the three main aspects of the United Nations' role in complex emergencies – humanitarian, political and military – can compete with and threaten to compromise each other. In practice, it is usually the humanitarian agenda which suffers.[23]

If civil-military relations are to be maintained effectively, humanitarian concerns must have an equal stake in the command structure and its decision-making.

Technical Relationships: Competence and Competition

If security relationships between civilian organizations and the military hinge on consent and distance, civil-military technical relationships are characterized by issues of competence and competition. Technical relationships between military forces and civilian humanitarian organizations come into play when the military are required to become relief providers. In such roles, the two groups find themselves:

> treading the same path and even treading on one another's toes.[24]

In these situations, civil-military relations have sometimes been strained, even acrimonious. Many civilian agencies, while respecting the huge logistical capacity of certain military forces (most notably that of the United States), have seriously criticized the technical capability of these forces in the provision of health, water and infrastructure. Their criticism is directed towards three main areas, where they find it hard to respect the humanitarian competence of most military forces: technical appropriateness, method and cost.

Inappropriate Capability and Expertise

Many civilian humanitarians have noted that the military are very good at providing health, water and infrastructure programmes for themselves, but that they are not best placed to do so for large populations of destitute people. The recent multi-donor Rwanda Evaluation, for example, has noted how Oxfam's water system was far more appropriate to conditions in Goma than that put in place by the US military.[25] Health agencies have also questioned the appropriateness of military medical staff and equipment to deal with the health needs of large numbers of destitute people.

Such criticisms – which have occasionally been levelled in a fairly frank manner in the field – are now well-known. However, it would be wrong to suppose that military personnel are not aware of their own distinctive competence. Their water, health and infrastructure capabilities are still primarily configured for war-fighting, and many soldiers who have been exposed to humanitarian operations are only too aware of how they would have to be adapted to be better suited for relief work.[26] In some of the criticisms made by civilian agencies, therefore, there is perhaps a tendency to shoot the messengers, rather than the governments who send and resource them – usually at extremely short notice.

But if it is generally true that, as in Iraq and Goma, civilian agencies tended to have a far better understanding of humanitarian assistance than military forces,[27] the fact remains that civilian humanitarian organizations have never shown themselves able to match the military in the speed of their initial response. At start-up in massive, rapid-onset emergencies, therefore, there is still reason to believe that military forces can play a priming role. This would obviously change – as has been argued for decades – if governments sufficiently resourced the stand-by capacity of the more appropriate civilian relief organizations. However, in Britain at least the recent Reserve Forces Bill signals that government policy continues to resist investment in civilian agency preparedness by enhancing military humanitarian preparedness instead.

A Non-developmental Approach

A further area of strain in the civil-military technical relationship concerns operational approaches. Most civilian humanitarian organizations have a definite developmental advantage over international military forces. Their network of local staff and their contacts with communities combine with their developmental expertise to make them better placed than military units to implement development activities. If the military's capability is expensive and inappropriate, so too, perhaps, are their methods and objectives. Civilian organizations observe that in the implementation of relief work, military forces are generally non-developmental and non-participatory. The approach of most armies, in particular to infrastructure such as wells, schools and clinics, is to do something for people rather than

with them, and not to think much about the long-term management
implications of what they construct or repair. It may also be argued that
military objectives in such projects are as much about public relations and
the maintenance of consent than about genuine development. A section of
the British Army manual, which calls such initiatives 'civil affairs projects',
illustrates this point:

> Winning the hearts and minds of the local population by a sustained
> civil affairs programme can transform the security environment and
> permit the safe accomplishment of a wide range of tasks inherent to
> Wider Peacekeeping operations…civil affairs projects may embrace a
> wide range of activities within local communities including medical
> and veterinary care, the provision and distribution of water, waste
> disposal, electrical power…the construction and development of
> schools…Commanders should allocate generous resources to civil
> affairs projects. The hearts and minds returns will amply justify such
> investments.[28]

To be fair to the British Army, the same section also urges close co-
operation with NGOs in such projects; but the fact that such projects have a
primary security objective rather than a developmental one is still evident.

Civilian agency doubts about the appropriateness of military methods in
relief and rehabilitation work run deep and reveal a concern about the time
perspective of most military missions. Most civilian agencies regard
military operations as short-termist in contrast to their own more forward
looking approach. Randel has noted:

> a fundamental difference between the mission-led approach of the
> military, who have specific tasks to achieve, and the longer term
> approach of many NGOs, who believe that the underlying principles
> of humanitarian assistance should be those of enabling people to get
> out of a situation on their terms.[29]

NGOs are only too well aware that it is usually they, and more importantly,
the communities with which they work, who will have to live with the
consequences of inappropriate cultural, social, political or material
'solutions' provided by the military. They suspect that the military will be
long gone when the bore-hole pump needs spare parts, or the 'interim' local
councils they set up descend into open conflict.

Nevertheless, for civilian agencies simply to single out the military for
special criticism in terms of being insensitive to developmental approaches
would be rather unfair. After all, the only reason that civilian agencies are
so aware of these issues is because they have made so many mistakes
themselves and indeed continue to do so on a regular basis. UN agencies

and international NGOs are also quite capable of being anti-developmental in their relief programmes.

Cost

Another civilian criticism of military relief capability concerns cost. Civilian organizations, supported by the recent findings of the Rwanda Evaluation, all argue that their own operations offer much better value for money than the military. Quite simply, civilian organizations, particularly NGOs, claim that they are not only better, but cheaper than the military.

Political Suspicion

If appropriate expertise is a feature of the civilian-military debate about technical competence, so too is competition. Much of the tension in the technical relationship can be read as competition:

> the civilian relief establishment may fear that the military is increasingly becoming the organization of choice for the international community in complex emergencies.[30]

UNHCR's official line on co-operating with the military has been to recommend a policy of mutual deference:

> Members of the military are asked...to defer to [civilian] humanitarian expertise, in the same way that humanitarian agencies should defer to the expertise of the military on security issues.[31]

Such a policy seems sensible, but may not be so easy to live by when governments are increasingly offering their military forces as relief providers or, as has been seen, when civilian agencies sometimes find international military tactics inappropriate. Deference cannot overcome genuine differences.

The sense of competition felt by civilian agencies is perhaps kindled by a suspicion regarding both donor and military motives behind increasing military humanitarianism. In its most extreme form, such suspicion of motives – principally Western – has extended to geopolitical conspiracy theories. Following on from the analysis of Rogers[32] and others, who see the lines of global conflict being redrawn from east-west to north-south, Stockton has talked of a 'creeping coup' through which Western military forces are using military humanitarian operations as rehearsals for the projecting of power into developing world settings at short notice.[33] In a similar vein, it has been a common refrain for NGOs in particular to accuse Western armies of jumping on the humanitarian band wagon in order to find a new role and so fend off further budget cuts.

The extent to which either of these suspicions is true is best decided by

political analysts. However, there is undoubtedly some important political
capital to be made by all governments out of the new humanitarian and
peacekeeping roles of their armed forces. As Randel points out:

> foreign ministries find that peacekeeping can offer much in the
> national interest – whether it is the opportunity to punch above one's
> weight on the SC or the foreign exchange generated by contributing
> troops to UN operations.[34]

But it would be wrong to assume that all military policy makers are leaping
on a peace-operations band wagon. Many have strong reservations about
their new role. Many military strategists are concerned that armies are
losing sight of their primary war-fighting role. The British officer General
Michael Rose is fond of observing that 'too much peacekeeping is bad for
soldiers', while there is similar concern in the US Army that an excess of
peace operation roles will take the fighting edge off soldiers.[35]

Social and Economic Impact

The social and the economic impact of a military presence in the field has
been another area of tension in the military-civilian relationship. Depending
on their scale, international military operations may have a massive impact
on the local economy. They soon become a major employer and a major
contractor in local economies, but there are losses as well as gains in the
economic opportunities they present. Inflated pay scales are often a by-
product of military operations. New jobs and income are often life-saving in
such situations, but they may also set precedents which are hard for more
indigenous parts of the economy to match. A brain-drain may become a
major feature of the economy through which the most able human resources
are attracted away from government and social services to work with the
military. Temporary, and perhaps long-term, disempowerment of some
national and local institutions may follow.

Economic opportunity may also develop into exploitation. The rise in
prostitution, which has accompanied several international military
operations, has been noted by a number of civilian agencies ranging from
local groups up to UNICEF itself. The UN Transitional Authority in
Cambodia (UNTAC), the UN Operation in Mozambique (ONUMOZ) and
UNPROFOR in the Former Yugoslavia have been particularly criticized for
contributing to a sexually-exploitative economy.

Yet the military are certainly not the only organization which impacts
upon the local economy and society. As many evaluations of humanitarian
programmes show, all civilian relief agencies have a similar effect. Civilian
relief agencies have been contributing to parallel economies for years. Also,
relief agencies cannot stand immune from charges of sexual exploitation,

although the differences in scale are obviously significant. The impact of a largely male military force, often thousands strong, will be greater than the impact of smaller, mixed staff contingents from civilian organizations. Nevertheless, this whole question of distorted social and economic impact may be another example of an operational issue in which civil-military organizations have more in common than they currently acknowledge. Both parties could work on common strategies to mitigate the negative effects of their presence.

Conclusion

Several conclusions may be drawn from this examination of civil-military relations. The first is that it would be unwise to stereotype military or civilian contingents operating in peace operations and to over-emphasize their differences. Both groups have more in common than is popularly suggested. They have shared perspectives on the limits of humanitarianism and they experience similar operational dilemmas in the management of consent during conflicts. Furthermore, while civilian humanitarian organizations must be reckoned to have a developmental advantage, both groups need to be concerned about the socio-economic impact of their presence and need to find ways of operating developmentally in protracted emergencies to mitigate the negative aspects of their intervention.

There is, in short, a common agenda which calls for more systematic conferring between the two parties. A more concerted effort to integrate joint training programmes and policy making should be encouraged. One obvious objective in such joint initiatives would be a working towards common standards of good practice within and between civilian and military operations. From this might emerge a transparent code of conduct to guide civil-military relations in peace operations.

NOTES

1. See I. Smillie, *The Alms Bazaar: Altruism under Fire – Non-Profit Organizations and International Development*, London: Intermediate Technology, 1995, Ch.6.
2. See H. Slim, 'The Continuing Metamorphosis of the Humanitarian Practitioner: Some New Colours for an Endangered Chameleon', *Disasters*, Vol.19, No.2, 1995, pp.119–20.
3. J. Benthall, *Disasters, Relief and the Media*, London: I.B. Tauris, 1993, p.174.
4 M. Junod, *Warrior without Weapons*, London: Cape, 1951; cited from 1982 ICRC edn, Geneva, p.33.
5. British Army advertisement on the overseas pages of the *Guardian*, 12 Jan. 1996, p.15, with the headline 'Could you be ready to work anywhere on this page within 24 hours?'
6. R. Connaughton, 'Military Support and Protection for Humanitarian Assistance: Rwanda, April-December 1994', Occasional Paper No.18, Strategic and Combat Studies Institute, Camberley, 1996, p.15.

7. R. Connaughton, 'Peacekeeping and Military Intervention', Occasional Paper No.3, Strategic and Combat Studies Institute, Camberley, 1992, p.39.
8. A. Natsios, 'NGOs and the UN System in Complex Humanitarian Emergencies: Conflict or Co-operation?', *Third World Quarterly*, Vol.16, No.3, 1995, p.410.
9. A phrase used by UN Secretary-General Boutros Boutros-Ghali in his Cyril Foster Lecture, Oxford University, Jan. 1996.
10. A. Donini, 'The Bureaucracies and the Free Spirits: Stagnation and Innovation in the Relationship between UN and NGOs', *Third World Quarterly*, Vol.16, No.3, 1995, p.421.
11. Natsios (n.8), p.406.
12. Ibid.
13. I am grateful to Toby Lanzer (previously of UNDHA Angola) for this British footballing image which accurately conjures up the state of the international NGO sector.
14. H. Slim, 'Non-Governmental Organizations: a Guide for the Military', in J. Mackinley (ed.), *Peace Support Operations: a Guide*, Providence, RI: Brown University, p.69.
15. Donini (n.10), p.32.
16. H. Slim and A. Penrose, 'UN Reform in a Changing World: Responding to Complex Emergencies', in J. Macrae and A. Zwi (eds.), *War and Hunger: Rethinking International Responses to Complex Emergencies*, London: Zed Books/Save the Children Fund UK, 1994, p.69.
17. See D. Bryer, 'Learning the Lessons from Bosnia', paper delivered at All Souls College, Oxford, 1 Mar. 1996; and M. Rose, speaking in a debate at Oxford Brookes University, Oxford, 13 Nov. 1995.
18. Connaughton (n.6), p.16.
19. See T. Weiss, 'Military-Civilian Humanitarianism: the Age of Innocence Is Over', *International Peacekeeping*, Vol.2, No.2, 1995.
20. See 'Initial Conclusions of the Conference on Conflict, Development and Military Intervention: the Role, Position and Experience of NGOs', organized by Liaison Committee of Development NGOs to the European Community, Brussels, 8–9 Apr. 1994.
21. Weiss (n.19), p.168.
22. Bryer (n.17), p.9.
23. The United Nations and Humanitarian Assistance, Save the Children Position Paper, London, Apr. 1994, p.3.
24. J. Randel, 'Aid, the Military and Humanitarian Assistance: an Attempt to Identify Recent Trends', *Journal of International Development*, Vol.6, No.3, 1994, p.336.
25. 'The International Response to Conflict and Genocide: Lessons from the Rwanda Experience', Steering Committee of Joint Evaluation of Emergency Assistance to Rwanda, 1996, Section 3, p.58.
26. T. Sharp, Y. Yip and J. Malone, 'US Military Forces and Emergency International Humanitarian Assistance', *Journal of the American Medical Academy*, Vol.272, No.5, 1994, pp.386-90.
27. US Army, 'Operation Provide Comfort: Lessons Learned – Observations', Fort Bragg, NC: John F. Kennedy Special Warfare Center, p.7.
28. British Army, *Wider Peacekeeping*, London: HMSO, 1995, pp.5–7.
29. Randel (n.24), p.337.
30. Slim (n.2), p.120.
31. UNHCR, *A UNHCR Handbook for the Military on Humanitarian Operations*, Geneva, 1995, p.33.
32. See P. Rogers, 'A Jungle Full of Snakes? Power, Poverty and International Security', in Tansey *et al* (eds.), *A World Divided: Militarism and Development after the Cold War*, London: Earthscan, 1994, pp.1–26.
33. N. Stockton, 'An NGO Perspective on Civil Reconstruction', paper presented at the Refugee Studies Programme Conference on the Role of the Military in Humanitarian Emergencies, Oxford University, Oct. 1995.
34. Randel (n.24), p.341.
35. Personal communication.

For Product Safety Concerns and Information please contact our EU
representative GPSR@taylorandfrancis.com
Taylor & Francis Verlag GmbH, Kaufingerstraße 24, 80331 München, Germany

www.ingramcontent.com/pod-product-compliance
Ingram Content Group UK Ltd.
Pitfield, Milton Keynes, MK11 3LW, UK
UKHW021632240425
457818UK00018BA/376